Edwar

5/11

NICK HERN BOOKS

LONDON

www.nickhernbooks.co.uk

A Nick Hern Book

5/11 first published in Great Britain as a paperback original
in 2005 by Nick Hern Books Limited, 14 Larden Road,
London W3 7ST

5/11 copyright © 2005 Edward Kemp
Introduction copyright © 2005 Edward Kemp

Edward Kemp has asserted his right to be identified
as the author of this work

Cover image: Daniel Abelson (Guy Fawkes)
Photography by Clare Park

Typeset by Country Setting, Kingsdown, Kent CT14 8ES
Printed in Great Britain by Cox and Wyman, Reading, Berks

A CIP catalogue record for this book is available from
the British Library

ISBN-13   978 1 85459 900 1
ISBN-10   1 85459 900 3

Introduction

5/11 is a fiction based on an event that did not take place.

The absence of an event – the King and Government did not
fall victims to a terrorist attack in 1605 – makes this particular
cornerstone of English history even shakier than most and
means that the Powder Plot (as it was known in its day) has
been the subject of almost every imaginable conspiracy theory
since, well, Tuesday afternoon, November 5th 1605. The only
incontrovertible fact anyone can agree on is that thirteen men
and two Jesuit priests were killed or executed in 1606 for their
involvement in an alleged conspiracy to blow up the Palace of
Westminster the previous year. Everything else is up for grabs.

Whose orders were they acting on? How did they gain access
to the Palace? Who supplied the gunpowder? Was there any
gunpowder? Each of these questions will lead the researcher
into a thicket of speculation, biased narratives and paper trails
that break off abruptly. An objective historian needs to
acknowledge these unstable foundations; the dramatist requires
something he can build on. This account of the last moments
of the reign of Queen Elizabeth and the first years of King
James is my own, it makes small claim to documentary, nor is
it entirely fanciful. I know pretty well what I've invented and
where I've used dramatic licence to conflate or compress
action too complicated or prolix to stage. The characters nearly
all have at least one foot in historical truth and many quote
their historical models. Their actions too are largely based on
what one can glean in the cracks between the various shades
of bias in the accounts. Where their motivations are ambivalent
I have endeavoured to preserve and dramatise this uncertainty.

What interests me as much as the activities of a group of
thirteen young men in 1605 are the recurring patterns which
may link them to nineteen young men in 2001, or four young
men in 2005, or thirteen young men in the early years of the
first millennium, or any number of the disillusioned or the dis-
possessed who have chosen to use religion to bind themselves
together in blood. The very unreasonableness of faith, which

can be its great glory in speaking truth to power, has too often made its own assertions of authority particularly barbaric. Christianity's peculiar success in conquering pain and death, turning defeat in this world into transcendent victory, has led certain strands of the faith into an obsession with these two human absolutes and with martyrdom as the highest witness to God's presence in the world. The very imperviousness to suffering that the early Christians showed in the arena before the lions – and which so impressed the Romans that they embraced the religion as their own – is what we now find so frightening in the face of the *jihadi*.

5/11 attempts to dramatise a story of ambivalent motives, of actions and words intentionally or unintentionally obscure, of equivocation, interpretation and misinterpretation, of the impact of faith on pain and charisma upon authority, played out in a country trying to find an identity for itself in a world where the border between religion and the state is being redrawn.

I am grateful to Chichester Festival Theatre for commissioning this play when it was little more than a title, to Steven Pimlott for his insight and guidance during the writing of it and the expertise and bravura he has brought to the staging, to an indomitable company of actors, many of whom accepted parts which were barely sketched, and to my family who have endured my obsession.

Edward Kemp
Chichester, July 2005

Edward Kemp

Edward Kemp is a writer, director and dramaturg. He has adapted Moliere's *Le Malade Imaginaire* and *Dom Juan* for the West Yorkshire Playhouse, the medieval *Mysteries* for the RSC and BBC Radio, W.G. Sebald's *The Emigrants* for BBC Radio, and *Nathan the Wise* and Bulgakov's *The Master and Margarita* for Chichester Festival Theatre. His adaptation of Faulkner's *As I Lay Dying* has been seen at the Young Vic, London, and in Louisiana and Los Angeles. Work with his own company, The Table Show, has played at the National Theatre, London, Edinburgh, Leeds, Budapest and Wellington, New Zealand. He has also written over a dozen short opera libretti.

Playing Notes

Scene and act divisions are, to an extent, arbitrary. The play
should run almost seamlessly in two halves, allowing
maximum collision and interplay between its many facets.
It is neither wholly in earnest nor entirely playful. Its language
is predominantly modern – though laced with many different
Englishes – whether its staging should also be modern I do not
know. It can be played by any number of actors, but ideally at
least thirteen.

An oblique slash (/) indicates the point of entry of the next
speaker. The absence of a full stop indicates either that the next
speaker interrupts or, if there is no capital letter beginning the
next speech, that there is a continuous flow of thought amongst
speakers. Italicised Latin text is intended to be sung.

*This text went to press before the end of rehearsals so may
differ slightly from the play as performed.*

5/11 was commissioned by and first performed at the Chichester Festival Theatre on 12 August 2005, with the following cast:

CECIL	Hugh Ross
CATESBY	Stephen Noonan
SOUTHWELL	Brendan O'Hea
ARCHBISHOP	Steven Beard
TOPCLIFFE	David Langham
KING JAMES	Alistair McGowan
QUEEN ANE	Annette McLaughlin
LENNOX	Aleksandar Mikic
LADY IN WAITING	Claire Parrish
THOMAS PERCY	Graham Turner
NORTHUMBERLAND	Raad Rawi
TRESHAM	Tom Silburn
MONTEAGLE	John Ramm
BROMLEY	Christian Bradley
ANNE VAUX	Fiona Dunn
MARTHA PERCY	Anna Francolini
EDWARD PERCY	Ollie Porter
HENRY GARNET	Richard O'Callaghan
SUFFOLK	Alexia Healy
WINTER	Mark Meadows
LIZZIE	Kay Curram
ELLESMERE	Brendan O'Hea
SOMERSET	Kieran Hill
JACK WRIGHT	Grant Anthony
KIT WRIGHT	Gary Milner
GUY FAWKES	Daniel Abelson

Director   Steven Pimlott
Designer   Ashley Martin-Davis
Lighting Designer   Chris Ellis
Composer   Jason Carr
Sound Designer   Matt McKenzie
Movement Director   Toby Sedgwick

Edward Kemp

The Burning Babe

Robert Southwell

As I in hoary winter's night stood shivering in the snow,
Surprised I was with sudden heat which made my heart to glow;
And lifting up a fearful eye to view what fire was near,
A pretty babe all burning bright did in the air appear;
Who, scorched with excessive heat, such floods of tears did shed
As though his floods should quench his flames which with his
    tears were fed.
'Alas,' quoth he, 'but newly born in fiery heats I fry,
Yet none approach to warm their hearts or feel my fire but I!
My faultless breast the furnace is, the fuel wounding thorns,
Love is the fire, and sighs the smoke, the ashes shame and scorns;
The fuel justice layeth on, and mercy blows the coals,
The metal in this furnace wrought are men's defiled souls,
For which, as now on fire I am to work them to their good,
So will I melt into a bath to wash them in my blood.'
With this he vanished out of sight and swiftly shrunk away,
And straight I called unto mind that it was Christmas Day.

from *St Peter's Complaint*, 1595

Characters

JAMES, *King of Scotland, then Britain*
ANE, *his wife*
ARCHBISHOP *of Canterbury* (*'Lol'*)
Earl of NORTHUMBERLAND (*'Harry'*)
Earl of LENNOX (*'Es'*)
Baron ELLESMERE, *Lord Treasurer*
Lord SOMERSET, *Lord Admiral*
Sir Robert CECIL, *Secretary to the Privy Council*
Sir Richard TOPCLIFFE, *Chief Justice* (*'Dicky'*)
Katherine SUFFOLK, *a lady of the English court*
BROMLEY, *a Pursuivant*

William MONTEAGLE
LIZZIE Monteagle, *his wife*
Francis TRESHAM, *her brother*
Robert CATESBY, *his cousin*
Thomas WINTER, *his cousin*
ANNE VAUX, *their cousin and Garnet's companion*
Thomas PERCY, *Northumberland's cousin*
MARTHA Percy, *his wife*
EDWARD Percy, *his son*
JACK Wright
KIT Wright, *his brother*

Henry GARNET, *Jesuit Superior in England*
Robert SOUTHWELL, *a Jesuit priest*

Guy FAWKES, *Ensign in the Spanish army*

PURSUIVANTS, *a* PAGEANT MASTER,
MEMBERS OF THE PRIVY COUNCIL, CONSPIRATORS,
HUNTING PACKS, *and others*

ACT ONE

Scene One

Darkness.

The rasp of a breath – in – out.

A bed. Upon it a body – little more than bones in an orange wig. Squatting at the bed's edge, a hunch-backed figure: ROBERT CECIL. *He is always watching. Now he addresses us.*

CECIL. In truth the King never dies. The King is dead, the cry goes up – Long live the King. Continuity – Tradition – The line unbroken to the crack of doom – English things.

As he continues to speak, CATESBY, *dressed in red (as he always will be) emerges bearing a bundle, which is a child in his arms. He lays it on the ground.*

In truth of course kings do die – some childless – and in the days of their passing, the hours grow thick – shadows walk – and hope is reckless.

CATESBY *sets light to the bundle. It burns with instant ferocity and at once the space is crowded. At the centre of the crowd a pale young man in a white shift stands on a cart. There are knives amongst the onlookers and burning braziers. The pale young man speaks. The crowd is volatile.*

SOUTHWELL. I am come to perform the last act of this miserable life. Almighty God, pardon and forgive me all my sins – as You are my witness, I never intended any evil against Her Majesty

ARCHBISHOP. Do you deny you are a priest of Rome?

SOUTHWELL. No – but I am no enemy to the Queen.

ARCHBISHOP. Do you acknowledge her as your lawful prince?

SOUTHWELL. I do.

ARCHBISHOP. You did not say this at your trial

SOUTHWELL. because you did not seek a priest or a traitor – only blood – and you shall have it – freely as my mother gave it to me – and if it's not enough, there will come as many more as willing as myself.

TOPCLIFFE. If the King of Spain or the Pope entered this land by force, intending to establish the religion you claim to be the true Catholic faith – would you resist them?

SOUTHWELL. I am a priest – I may not fight.

ARCHBISHOP. Would you counsel others to defend Her Majesty?

SOUTHWELL. I would counsel all men to maintain the right of their prince.

TOPCLIFFE. And has the Queen no right to maintain our religion and to forbid yours?

SOUTHWELL. No – she does not.

ARCHBISHOP. So if the Pope came to establish your religion you would not defend the Queen against him? I charge you before this assembly and before God.

SOUTHWELL. I am a Catholic priest, your Grace – I would never fight – nor counsel others to fight against my religion – O Christ, I will never deny you for a thousand lives.

TOPCLIFFE. Robert Southwell / – you are a traitor to Her Majesty Queen Elizabeth, Queen of England, Wales, Ireland and France. Carry out the sentence.

SOUTHWELL. 'Whether we live, we live unto the Lord: or whether we die, we die unto the Lord. Therefore, whether we live or whether we die, we are the Lord's.'

A noose is lowered. SOUTHWELL *kisses it and it is placed around his neck.*

Domine, in manus tuas, commendo spiritum meum.

The cart is pulled away – the body dangles. He looks upwards, beatific, and repeats 'In manus tuas, commendo spiritum meum.'

In another place CECIL *is going over accounts. Although they are not in the same location,* CECIL *and* TOPCLIFFE *talk to each other.*

CECIL. Coals, sixpence; horse to bear him to the gallows, twelvepence; wright's axe for heading, four shillings.

TOPCLIFFE. Cut him down.

The crowd move in.

CECIL. Leave him. Hand axe and cutting knife for ripping and quartering, fourteen pence.

TOPCLIFFE. Leave him longer he'll be dead.

CECIL. Leave him. Four hooks for hanging the quarters on the four gates, three shillings and eightpence. A mason for setting the hooks in the gates, tenpence a day. Fire and coals for melting the lead to set the hooks, eightpence.

The body's movements have stopped.

Take him down.

A swarm of people gather around the body as it is brought down.

TOPCLIFFE. Getting soft, Cecil. Your father would never have shown a Jesuit such tenderness.

CECIL. My father knew the English animal, Topcliffe – so does the Queen. We're an island people – the sea has got into our blood – we rush to violence and then yearn for fair play. I hate a Jesuit like any man –

The EXECUTIONER *rips the heart out of the body and holds it aloft.*

but let the Pope make his saints – he doesn't need our assistance.

Scene Two

Continuous. A stag charges into the space followed by a yelping, barking chase. KING JAMES *kills the stag, smearing his face with blood. He wears armour.* QUEEN ANE *is there with her women. She is pregnant.* THOMAS PERCY *waits.*

JAMES. Look at him, Annie – what a brute – Killed him, I did – wi' these hands. Tell her, Es.

LENNOX. Pierced him through the heart.

JAMES. Jes like I did ma Annie – eh? So tell – which would you rather in your bed? King Stag or King Jimmy?

ANE. The one which will be King of England.

JAMES *has a fit of coughing;* ANE *moves towards him.*

You should take off this

JAMES. Dinna touch my / armour

ANE. it makes your chest bad

JAMES. Don' fecking mother me – thirty-five years no mother – I dinna need one now. I'm sorry – I'm sorry. Mea culpa. Come here, ma wee Danish broodmare. (*He kisses her.*) When I wear the English croon, Annie – your wardrobe will make any Queen in Europe weep – you'll glide on silk – our bairns one wee row o'cygnies behind their mither swan. (*He strokes her belly.*) What is it? Lad or lassie?

ANE. I think it is a girl.

JAMES. Not a boy?

ANE. I have given you boys already – I want a girl for myself. But I will call her for you – I will call her Mary for your mother.

JAMES. No. Call her Elizabeth – and make sure the barren biddy kens it.

PERCY. Her Majesty is at death's door.

JAMES. Will somebiddy no' open it for her? No, I never said that – naebiddy heard me say that. Guid Queen Bess – I love her as ma ain . . . well, May she live for ever – and knowing ma luck she probably will. No – I never said – Who are you anyway?

PERCY. Thomas Percy.

JAMES. I ken that – you told me. Earl of Northumberland's man.

PERCY. I served the Earl my cousin against the Spanish in Flanders. He is eager to see Your Majesty on the English throne.

JAMES. Och, that's what they all say, dinne, Esme?

LENNOX. Aye, Percy, but how will the Earl oil the King's passage?

JAMES. Forgive Esme – he's picked up a certain Gallic laxness.

PERCY. The Catholics of England look to Your Majesty's

reign as a new era of hope for the one million souls of the faithful now suffering persecution.

ANE. One million?

LENNOX. Could be handy in a scrap, boss.

JAMES. There's no gonna be a scrap.

PERCY. Should Queen Elizabeth die without naming a successor, the Earl of Northumberland pledges the support of all Catholic gentry in respect of your claim

JAMES. Will everybiddy no' talk like I was some prentice puling for a partnership. It's no' a claim – God fingered me.

PERCY. There's not a Catholic who'd dispute it.

Elsewhere, NORTHUMBERLAND *is watching.*

JAMES. Percy, when you fought alongside Flanders Protestants against the Catholic King of Spain – who were you fighting for?

PERCY. I was defending my country, England

JAMES. against your brother Catholics

PERCY. against a foreign power

JAMES. Did that no' pain you?

PERCY. My loyalty is to England and my King.

JAMES. I know your pain, Thomas Percy – it is mine – and it is ma destiny to bring peace to the factious children of Britain – only I can do this – not only King of Scotland and richtful heir to the English croon – but Protestant son of a Catholic Queen.

PERCY. The Queen of Scots is an inspiration to all those who now suffer under the heel of / the oppressor.

JAMES. Aye, aye – her persecutions were yours and her persecutors were the same. Ma Annie, she's a Catholic too – did you no' know that? – She gets letters from the Pope – Percy, if a man gives good service, I don't much care where he worships. All I say is – avoid the extremities – keep to the middle path – that's the British way.

PERCY *steps out of the scene with* JAMES *and talks to* NORTHUMBERLAND. *Meanwhile* JAMES *and party begin to exit.*

PERCY. And then he took me by the hand and said, 'It's the King's pleasure that the Earl of Northumberland give the Catholics hope they should be well dealt with.' He wrote you this.

JAMES. How'd I do, Es?

LENNOX. Cecil couldnae done better, boss.

PERCY. It's not all – Prince Harry is going to be raised in the true faith.

N'LAND. James said that?

PERCY. No – the Queen – after he'd gone.

JAMES. You nivir?

ANE. Do you want the Crown of England or not?

JAMES. Saucy minx.

ANE. Will you come to my chamber tonight?

JAMES. Och, it's full moon – I promised Esme we'll stalk badger.

They've gone. PERCY *and* NORTHUMBERLAND *are left alone.* CECIL *is watching from another place.*

PERCY. It's good, isn't it?

N'LAND. Sorry?

PERCY. The letter.

N'LAND. Mm

PERCY. The world is changing – I mean, I don't think I ever believed I'd – and now here I am – he took me by the hand – It's good news, isn't it? – am I grinning?

N'LAND. Like a loon, cousin. Yes – he's given us hope – but for the time being I think we should keep this between ourselves.

PERCY. Of course – absolutely – Why?

N'LAND. Because if the judges – or the bishops – or the Commons know that James favours emancipation, even toleration, they will fight his claim tooth and claw.

PERCY. Mum's the word.

As PERCY *leaves* NORTHUMBERLAND, CECIL *steps into the scene.*

CECIL (*taking the letter*). Whom will he tell?

As NORTHUMBERLAND *names them, one by one they join* PERCY. *The two scenes run simultaneously –* CECIL *and* NORTHUMBERLAND *in one place;* PERCY, CATESBY, TRESHAM *and* MONTEAGLE *in another.*

N'LAND. Robert Catesby – Catesby's cousin Francis Tresham – Tresham's brother-in-law William Monteagle

CECIL. and from them all Catholic England

N'LAND. All one million of them?

CECIL. Yes, well, that little invention served its purpose, didn't it?

MONTEAGLE. You great dupe, Perce. Why didn't you go down on all fours and let the old queer bugger you?

PERCY. He shook this hand

MONTEAGLE. put it on his dick

PERCY. You believe me, don't you, Francis?

TRESHAM. I'd like to, Perce – I'd like to

PERCY. You don't have to agree with Monteagle all the time – he's married to your sister, not you.

MONTEAGLE. Admit it, sweaty – James has duped you – you've been duped by a shirt-lifter.

PERCY. He's going to convert – I saw it in his eyes

MONTEAGLE. When, sweaty, when is he?

TRESHAM. On his death-bed – like they all do

CATESBY. She won't – she'll seek no last-minute consolation – our devil queen will go to the bonfire with all her crimes upon her – to keep us smarting while she rots.

PERCY. But you believe we can trust James, don't you, Cat?

CATESBY. What did Northumberland say?

PERCY. He said

N'LAND. Are you sure we're doing the right thing?

PERCY. he said he thought it was good

CECIL. Have you got an alternative, Harry? Another fifty years of endless, pointless strife

MONTEAGLE. Spain's our only hope

CATESBY. then we have no hope

CECIL. wars which drain the country of youth and wealth

TRESHAM. nobody wants a king imposed by wops, Monty

CECIL. burning our ships, slaughtering our merchants

MONTEAGLE. I'm not asking them to invade, Francis

CATESBY. another Armada, another thousand men, trashed on the coast of Scotland

CECIL. the fields of Flanders drenched with English blood

MONTEAGLE. I want them to give us arms, money, horses – a revolt

CATESBY. English Catholicism has been an expensive hobby for the Spanish Crown.

CECIL/PERCY. And James will give us peace.

N'LAND/MONTEAGLE. He's a foreigner

CATESBY. The King of Spain's a foreigner.

MONTEAGLE. he's a slippery Scot who'd piss on his mother's grave to get the crown. And a poofter to boot.

CECIL. My ancestors were Welsh peasants. People forget these things.

CATESBY. So – Monty wants the King of Spain – Perce wants the Queen of Scotland – Francis, who do you want to sell us to?

TRESHAM. Me? – anyone who'll give us toleration.

CATESBY. Toleration – or freedom?

MONTEAGLE. Spain will make us free – Spain will make England Catholic once more

PERCY. and Spanish.

MONTEAGLE. Better a Spanish Catholic than buggered by a Protty Scot.

PERCY *launches at* MONTEAGLE.

CATESBY. Francis.

They separate them.

Cocks away, boys.

PERCY. I'm going home. I'm going somewhere where people haven't forgotten how to hope.

CATESBY. And we're coming with you.

PERCY. Why?

CATESBY. Because you've got Mr and Mrs Farmer staying with you.

PERCY. Mr Perkins and his sister

CATESBY. Whatever – we need to talk to him – he has something to show us.

They start to go.

TRESHAM. Who's Mr Perkins?

MONTEAGLE. Who d'you think, Francis? Father Garnet. Come on – keep up.

Gone. CECIL *and* NORTHUMBERLAND *are alone on stage.*

CECIL. You know, Harry, if there really were a million Catholics – you could be King. You've a good claim – and you're English – and loved by Catholics and Protestants alike

N'LAND. A foot in both graves. No – I know my place at the table.

CECIL. I think maybe you're right – I think we should keep this letter very safe – just in case James forgets what he's promised.

Scene Three

PERCY*'s house. Night.* BROMLEY *and other* PURSUIVANTS. ANNE VAUX, MARTHA PERCY. CECIL *elsewhere, watching.*

BROMLEY. There should be seven servants – any more, I want to know.

ANNE VAUX. It's the middle of the night – / what does this mean?

BROMLEY. Martha Percy?

MARTHA. I'm Martha Percy. Who are you?

BROMLEY. Your husband, Thomas Percy – where's he?

MARTHA. Away – on business.

ANNE VAUX. And what is your – business?

BROMLEY. I didn't get your name.

ANNE VAUX. Nor I yours.

MARTHA. This is my neighbour, Anne Perkins – she is staying with me while my husband is away.

BROMLEY (*sniffing around* ANNE VAUX). I can smell incense – can anyone else smell incense?

ANNE VAUX. It's soap – perhaps the scent is unfamiliar.

BROMLEY. Sharp ears, my boys – good noses. Sniffed out a priest last week – tucked up behind the panelling with his whore. (*Laughs.*) A box like this – what could you hide in that? A prayer book – a candle – a pyx?

Throws the box on the ground – it breaks open. It is empty.

But then you got to think what could be in the cracks – the cavities – where you could slip an agnus dei, an indulgence, a piece of the true cross.

Stamps it to bits.

CECIL (*watching*). So many secret places – in houses – in boxes – in bodies.

A PURSUIVANT *comes with a boy* (EDWARD).

PURSUIVANT. I found this under a bed.

BROMLEY. A whelp, Stevie – a little chicken – well done.

MARTHA (*to* EDWARD). Don't be frightened

BROMLEY. What's your name?

EDWARD. Edward Percy.

BROMLEY. Know the name Garnet, Edward?

EDWARD. No, sir.

BROMLEY. Never heard it?

EDWARD. No.

BROMLEY. D'you go to church?

EDWARD. Yes.

BROMLEY. You listen to the preacher?

EDWARD. Yes.

BROMLEY. What does he say happens to liars, Edward?

EDWARD. They burn in everlasting fire.

BROMLEY. They do – in everlasting fire and everlasting darkness. So – has there been a priest in this house? Think carefully, Edward – about the fire and the darkness.

EDWARD. I swear – on my immortal soul – there has been no priest in this house.

PERCY, CATESBY, MONTEAGLE *and* TRESHAM *arrive.*

PERCY. This is a late hour to come visiting, gentlemen

MONTEAGLE. An hour when all honest folk would be in their beds.

BROMLEY. We are servants of the Crown in search of priests

CATESBY. Why – to shrive your souls?

They attack – driving out the PURSUIVANTS.

PERCY. Get out – get out of my house – go back to whatever corner of hell spued you forth

MONTEAGLE. Vermin.

PERCY. Have they hurt you? Have they hurt any hair of you?

He embraces his family.

MARTHA. No – no – no harm.

CATESBY. Where's Garnet?

MARTHA. We bundled him down the second we heard the horses. We were about to start mass

ANNE VAUX (*at the trap*). And now the catch has broken.

PERCY. It can only be opened from the inside.

ANNE VAUX (*knocking*). Henry – Henry – it's Anne. They've gone. Father?

MONTEAGLE. Can he breathe in there?

PERCY. I don't know – yes – I'm sure.

ANNE VAUX. Henry.

> CATESBY *moves swiftly to the trap.*

CATESBY (*to* ANNE VAUX). Out of the way. Get out of my way.

ANNE VAUX. You'll hurt him.

CATESBY. And if he's dead? Francis.

> *They break the trap. It opens to reveal a body lying stretched out in white.*

ANNE VAUX. Henry

CATESBY. Father

MARTHA. O Holy Mary

> *The body lifts an arm.*

GARNET. Hand, somebody.

> TRESHAM *helps* GARNET *out.*

I thought they'd never leave. Must have nodded off. I was having the most lovely dream

ANNE VAUX. You – You deserve to get stuck

GARNET. Francis, William, Robert. Is it card night already? A drink, don't you think, Edward – after all the excitement. Why the serious faces? Nobody's hurt are they?

ANNE VAUX. Is that the point?

GARNET. Did they take much?

MARTHA. Only your supper.

GARNET. Then let us thank God, rejoice in the defeat of his enemies – and rustle up some bread and cheese.

CATESBY. We need to talk.

GARNET. Food first, morals later.

EDWARD (*pouring*). I did just what you taught me, Father – I met the heretic in the eye and said, 'No, there has been no priest in this house' and then in my head I said, 'Wearing a pink hat.'

GARNET. A pink hat, eh?

EDWARD. Was that a sin?

GARNET. No, no – I don't believe I've ever worn a pink hat –
n-not in this house anyway – so you're in the – c – c – c –
damn this –

His hand is shaking so much that EDWARD *can't pour.*

ANNE VAUX. Let me.

She takes the glass and fills it. Raises it to GARNET's
mouth. CATESBY *watches them. Meanwhile:*

MARTHA. They weren't the usual men

PERCY. Not local?

MONTEAGLE. It's what they do now – they farm it out. Nice
little earner for their friends.

GARNET (*to* ANNE VAUX). The prince of this world grows
desperate because he foresees his time will be short

MONTEAGLE. The Lords have sanctioned it – Cecil's inciting
it

ANNE VAUX (*to* GARNET). We should leave here

MONTEAGLE. I'll tell you – if I was in the Lords

GARNET. you'd spend more time in St Paul's Cathedral than
you do already – it's not only Cecil who has a hundred
eyes, William – you and Lizzie were there again last
Sunday

MONTEAGLE. We didn't take communion

GARNET. the thief is proud he does not murder his victim. So
– if it isn't cards, what's summoned you?

PERCY. I've been to Scotland, Henry – that's where
Northumberland sent me – I'm not meant to tell you this –
so keep it under your – I met King James – he shook this
hand – and promised us toleration. Looked me in the eyes
and said it. It's come.

Silence.

O sweet heaven – even you don't believe me.

GARNET. I do. I do, Percy. It's come.

CATESBY. So – will you publish the Brief now?

GARNET. Which brief?

CATESBY. Enough games.

GARNET. Rome sends me many briefs, / about many things

CATESBY. The Brief which says that when the bitch dies we should fight for a monarch who will show His Holiness due loyalty.

GARNET. It does not say fight, it says strive

CATESBY. which means fight

GARNET. which means go on as we have been – praying, converting, doing God's work in this realm.

MONTEAGLE. Can we all be included in this conversation?

GARNET. One year since, Rome dispatched a Brief for the English Laity, to be published at a time when I thought prudent.

PERCY. And what's it say?

GARNET. Percy, if I told you, I might as well publish it.

MONTEAGLE. So why's Catesby seen it?

CATESBY. If the Pope meant business as usual why did he bother to write at all?

MONTEAGLE. Why has Catesby seen it and we haven't?

GARNET. Rome is a long way away – I do not believe they fully understand our situation.

CATESBY. Please don't set yourself above the Pope.

MONTEAGLE. Why has this Brief been shown to him and not to

TRESHAM. Oh shut up, Monty – you know perfectly well – Cat's always been the favourite son

MONTEAGLE. Well, my damn secretary is at this moment talking to the Spanish Governor of Flanders – I want to know if the Pope approves

GARNET. Am I missing something – Has the Queen passed away while I've been down there?

CATESBY. She could die tomorrow – and James would become King.

GARNET. And then we should rejoice – because he has proved himself a good friend to the faithful.

CATESBY. The devil is always a friend to the faithful – how else would he lead them to damnation? That Brief is the word of the Pope to the people of this land – you have no right to keep it from us.

GARNET. I've every right to publish it at a moment I deem fit

CATESBY. And while you're fiddling with sets and inking syllables, the time's gone – Rome reckons what even Monty's grasped – this is the moment – when the clock stops between two reigns – that we could turn it back – and we are being stitched up.

GARNET. Whatever became of that trusting boy I once taught?

CATESBY. He saw the man who showed me the face of God in all His terror and magnificence turn into a fawning, lascivious old fop.

ANNE VAUX. How dare you

GARNET. Anne

ANNE VAUX. for twenty years he has lived like a fugitive

GARNET. Anne

ANNE VAUX. striving every hour to bring Christ into this godless world, not knowing if the next bright-eyed serving-girl wouldn't send him to the / gallows

GARNET. please, Anne

ANNE VAUX. if you won't defend yourself, I will – twenty years – who here hasn't he brought hope and comfort to – and love – oh go on, smile – but when you have suffered as he has – then come back and lecture him – boy

GARNET. We should go, Anne

MARTHA. You're leaving us

GARNET. I do not believe tonight was chance – I believe Cecil would love nothing more than to place my head before his dying queen. Take heart – he that is to come, will come – and if a little hope is too much vanity, I can only say – we all get old.

CATESBY. Not God. A hundred years in his sight is as nothing.

GARNET. Then let us learn from his endurance.

They leave. As they go, TRESHAM *is detained by* CECIL.

CECIL. Where's he going now? – Garnet or Perkins or Farmer?

TRESHAM. I don't know – I didn't know he was at Percy's until we came there.

CECIL. And this woman who travels with him? His whore

TRESHAM. She's not a whore.

CECIL. How would you know?

TRESHAM. Her name's Anne. Anne Vaux

CECIL. a cousin of yours

TRESHAM. she is

CECIL. but you have so many cousins. Tom Winter, for instance – Monteagle's secretary – why's he been sent to Flanders?

TRESHAM. I don't know – I am not my brother-in-law's keeper.

CECIL. You hired the boat for him.

TRESHAM. I didn't hire it, I paid for it

CECIL. With what? My money?

TRESHAM. I had to – Monteagle asked me –You don't understand the importance of the way things look

CECIL (*snapping*). I think I understand that better than most, Francis Tresham. Christ, you're damnall use as a spy, aren't you.

TRESHAM. Monteagle wants the Spanish Governor to provide aid – support – when the Queen dies – for a rising in the Midlands.

CECIL. I know this – like God I know everything you will ever tell me – but you still have to tell me or I send you to hell – or rather the Tower. Actually, I'm sending you to the Tower anyway.

TRESHAM. Why?

CECIL. The Queen's sick, you're heir to the largest Catholic estate in the country – do I need a reason? It's only till she dies. And all your old associates will be there – cousin Catesby, Mad Jack Wright, his equally mad brother Kit – help you keep up appearances

TRESHAM. What about bloody Monteagle?

CECIL. No – Monty's more useful in his kennel – someone needs to welcome Tom Winter back from Flanders.

TRESHAM *is led away.*

At MONTEAGLE's *house,* THOMAS WINTER *enters carrying a letter. He looks awkward.* MONTEAGLE *comes to him. Takes the letter.*

Meanwhile KATHERINE SUFFOLK *comes to* CECIL.

How was Flanders, Lady Katherine?

SUFFOLK. Deadly, Sir Robert.

CECIL. And the Spanish Governor?

SUFFOLK. Likewise. I've had more pleasure from a carrot.

CECIL. But not more pillowtalk, I trust.

She kisses him.

SUFFOLK. The Spanish won't contend James.

CECIL. Known or supposed?

SUFFOLK. Even if His Holiness required it. The war's costing the Governor personally a thousand guilders a month. He can't afford to clothe his wife – let alone a cardinal.

CECIL. But he could afford this. (*A large diamond ring.*)

SUFFOLK. For services rendered.

CECIL. And what does the Governor want rendered in return?

SUFFOLK. The Protestant insurgents – the ones you armed in Flanders

CECIL. allegedly

SUFFOLK. he wants you to get rid of them. He can't.

CECIL. I'm flattered.

SUFFOLK. Get rid of them – and he'll tell Madrid to agree the terms for peace – and give you ten per cent of the silk revenue.

CECIL. And what will he say to young Tommy Winter?

MONTEAGLE. Nothing?

SUFFOLK. The Governor's only son was in the Armada

WINTER. He pledged me His Catholic Majesty's prayerful pity for our plight – promised the matter his profoundest consideration – and begged to be informed

WINTER/SUFFOLK. inmediamente cuando la reina herética se haya muerto

MONTEAGLE. No money? No arms?

CECIL. No Andalucian bay to ride into battle

SUFFOLK. No Toledo steel engraved with the lives of the saints

CECIL. No blackwork cloak from Zaragoza.

WINTER. We could send to Rome – or ask the nuncio to talk to the Governor – Supposing Garnet wrote

MONTEAGLE. Garnet's backing James – the world's backing James.

WINTER. I would go back to Flanders whenever you asked.

MONTEAGLE. Flanders is finished, Tom.

CECIL. Tell the Governor twelve and he's got a deal.

> LIZZIE MONTEAGLE *comes to* MONTEAGLE *and* WINTER.

LIZZIE. William

MONTEAGLE. Ah good – dinner – Tom, you'll stay

WINTER. I was / going

MONTEAGLE. No, no, I need you – We've an important letter to write. Lizzie, can we lay an extra – what is it?

LIZZIE. They've arrested Francis.

MONTEAGLE. Your brother Francis?

LIZZIE. What other Francis? And Catesby and the Wrights.

MONTEAGLE. Then the end must be near. Tom – really, there's no time to waste

WINTER. I'm sorry, William, but I have to

MONTEAGLE. we must write to Scotland tonight –

LIZZIE. For God's sake, William, my brother is in the Tower – does that matter to you at all?

MONTEAGLE. Yes – I mean, of course – it's routine, kitten – the Queen's about to die, you see – and this is why we must write – the tide's turning – has turned – if we don't move, we'll be washed away – Francis too.

LIZZIE and MONTEAGLE *go.* WINTER *is left.*

Tom?

WINTER *goes.*

Scene Four

The ebb and flow of the Queen's breath grows.

CECIL *alone with the dying Queen.*

CECIL. It is the Vigil of the Annunciation – in old England the last day of the old year – the earth turns away from the sun – and when this night has passed, it will be a new year and a new England.

JAMES *appears with* LENNOX *in Scotland.*

JAMES. Are you superstitious, Es?

LENNOX. How do you mean, boss?

JAMES. Do you believe in fortune tellers, astrology, witches?

LENNOX. Do you, boss?

JAMES. There was a witch once whispered me the very words I said to Annie on our wedding night in Elsinore – how do you explain that?

LENNOX. Cecil had a spy under the bed?

JAMES (*laughs*). Aye – most like.

> GARNET *appears elsewhere with* ANNE VAUX. *He carries a candle, she a bowl of water. He still wears his ecclesiastical regalia that she slowly removes with great love.*

> Es – I think this will be the night she dies. Elizabeth. Coming o'er the hill there, I saw a cloud – feck it no – it was nae cloud – I saw a bloody head in the sky.

LENNOX. What – like a man?

JAMES. No – like a child – stillborn.

LENNOX. I saw nothing, boss.

JAMES. Ach – it was nothing – a fecking cloud. Hold me.

GARNET. Come and celebrate New Year with me

ANNE VAUX. No – New Year makes me sad

GARNET. because you look backwards – Let the old year go – In a few hours Gabriel will announce to Mary the joyful news of the coming of Our Saviour

ANNE VAUX. And it will be twenty springtimes since you and Southwell set foot in my father's house

GARNET. There were three Jesuits in England then – now they lock us up, we turn their prisons into seminaries

ANNE VAUX. so they rip you to pieces instead

> GARNET*'s hands are trembling.*

GARNET. Well God knows, I'd sooner twitch on the gallows than in my chamber

ANNE VAUX. Don't say that. Do you envy him?

GARNET. Southwell? He was my dearest companion – and Christ chose him for glory

ANNE VAUX. and there is no greater glory than the martyr's

GARNET. the pattern of Our Saviour's own sacrifice

ANNE VAUX. is it so much greater than leading His flock to safety? Can I ask you something

GARNET. You want to see the Brief from Rome.

GARNET *takes it from inside his clothes and gives it to her.*

CATESBY. Silence. As if all England hunched at its door listening to the tick tock of her slow passing. Catching its own breath as the spent lungs empty – and then inhale again. Not a bell has rung for days – not a bugle sounded – war and worship tongue-tied.

The Privy Council join CECIL *at the Queen's bedside.*

We see CATESBY *in his cell in the Tower.*

In the Tower we sleep two floors beneath the royal arsenal – a hundred thousand hogs of gunpowder dozing – enough to blow all England into smoke.

ARCHBISHOP. Your Majesty – You have been a great Queen upon earth, but you must shortly yield an account of your stewardship to the King of Kings. We who shall unhappily dwell in your absence must look to your legacy. We humbly ask Your Majesty to signify the candidate most worthy to succeed you.

TOPCLIFFE. Philip Habsburg, King of Spain

ANNE VAUX. What do you think they mean us to do?

GARNET. I don't think they know themselves.

TOPCLIFFE. Archduchess Isabella, the Infanta of Spain.

ANNE VAUX. You'll have to publish it sometime.

GARNET. and lend authority to Robert's wildness – I don't believe that's His Holiness' intention.

ANNE VAUX. So what will you do with it?

GARNET *takes the letter from her.*

GARNET. Rome is a long way away.

TOPCLIFFE. The Earl of Northumberland.

GARNET *holds the letter to the candle. It burns.*

Lady Arabella Stuart.

ANNE VAUX. Why do you never defend yourself? – when Catesby attacks you, why do you never defend yourself?

JAMES. Can I do this, Es?

GARNET. Because I hear my own words in Robert's mouth

LENNOX. You were born to be King – God chose you.

JAMES. Ay – and He never gets it wrong, does He.

ANNE VAUX. No – Robert is in love with death and you are not

LENNOX. If He did no' mean you to be King, would He have spared you so often?

ANNE VAUX. you are not

TOPCLIFFE. James Stuart, King of Scotland.

GARNET. Listen

CECIL. Did you see that, gentlemen?

GARNET. I heard something rustle.

N'LAND. She moved her hand.

GARNET. There – at the casement.

CECIL. Upon which name?

ANNE VAUX. What was it?

N'LAND. James Stuart.

GARNET. I think it was the wings of an angel.

She kisses his hand.

CECIL. Thank you, Your Majesty.

CATESBY. It is the darkest hour of the night.

The breathing stops.

ARCHBISHOP. The Queen is dead.

CECIL. Long live the King.

A cheer like a great wave.

ACT TWO

Scene One

Fanfares and bells. JAMES *makes his royal procession from Edinburgh to London. Crowds like choppy seas on a sunny day.* WINTER *stands outside it all watching.* CATESBY, *elsewhere, watches* WINTER.

WINTER. He left Edinburgh with two hundred Scots in tow. By Berwick – where he lay across the border to show how two kingdoms could exist in one body – half of them had knighthoods.

Three COUNCILLORS *watch* JAMES*'s progress.*

SOMERSET. He's going to make us all hold hands – I know it.

ELLESMERE. What do you mean?

SOMERSET. When he took power in Scotland he made all the warring nobility walk hand in hand through the streets of Edinburgh.

TOPCLIFFE. I'm not holding hands with any effing Jock.

ELLESMERE. What about a Papist?

The procession continues.

WINTER. At Newcastle the Catholic merchants filled every vessel in the city with wine and lit bonfires in celebration of his coming

PERCY. Mark my words – in a year he will have returned to Rome

WINTER. and William Monteagle was created a peer of the realm.

MONTEAGLE *is honoured by* JAMES.

TRESHAM. Why him – why bloody Monty?

The procession continues.

WINTER. At Newark a cutpurse who had been following the throng was arrested and executed on the King's command.

CECIL. Your Majesty, English law demands that the case is heard by a judge

JAMES. I heard it

CECIL. in a court of law

JAMES. I am the law.

CECIL. In England

JAMES. Sir Robert – your services to our cousin the late Queen are famous – and we look forward to your serving us in some great office – but it is the King who sits in the throne of God, and from God is all justice derived. Northumberland.

NORTHUMBERLAND *leads* JAMES *and* ANE *to their coronation.*

The Coronation of King James.

In his crown and robes the King addresses his people.

JAMES. A new dawn has broken. You know – folk of every sort have ridden, run, flown to welcome us to this place God has provided. How shall we repay you all? With empty promises? Och, we know those men – masters of the glib and oily arts – many fine words but no fine coin – I am not one – Believe me – I bring you no promises – I bring you blessings.

A strange call – like a baby or a bird.

The first blessing is peace. Since I first wore the crown of Scotland in my crib, never had I quarrel with any prince. This day is brought to end the great and tedious war with Spain that has sapped this nation's wealth and wasted its youth.

The call again.

You know – peace abroad is a great blessing – but it's as nothing to peace at home. In my blood two ancient and famous kingdoms – two twins bred in one belly – England and Scotland – hold sway.

The call twice.

But God made us one island, compassed by one sea, sharing one tongue – a little world within ourself, worthy once more to bear the name Britannia, the people of Brute. We shall have one coin, one law, one flag. The lion shall lie down with the / unicorn

The call again.

What the feck is that noise?

Scene Two

Snap change leaving JAMES, CECIL, SUFFOLK, ANE, LENNOX, NORTHUMBERLAND. *An object covered by a cloth.*

CECIL. It's a gift from the Spanish Governor – sign of good faith for the Treaty – I'm just sending it to the Tower.

ANE. What crime has it committed?

SUFFOLK. The Tower is the home of the Royal Menagerie, ma'am. It holds all manner of savage beasts – lions, estridges

N'LAND. Jesuits.

JAMES. Can I no' see what it is first?

CECIL. The Governor had been informed that you liked rare beasts

JAMES. I do.

The cage is uncovered.

What is it?

CECIL. It's called a doudou. It's from Africa.

JAMES. And what do you do with a doudou?

CECIL. Portuguese sailors consider the flesh a delicacy.

JAMES. When I sailed to fetch Annie in Elsinore I ate pickled sea snails – they said that was a delicacy too. Can it sing? Fly?

LENNOX. Mebbe you could hunt it.

ANE. It is the most disgusting thing I have ever seen.

The Dodo cries.

CECIL. Shall I drown it?

JAMES. It's a gift from the Spanish Crown

LENNOX. Two fingers from the Spanish Crown.

The Dodo cries.

JAMES. What did it say?

CECIL. It squawked.

JAMES. No – no, it said something. Listen.

No sound. JAMES *kicks the cage.*

Och go on, you fat dingus, give us a

The Dodo cries.

There – d'you hear that? Pax. It said pax.

CECIL. Pax?

JAMES. It's Latin for peace. It's a bird of peace, is what it is.
Sign of a new era – I mean, look at those wee babby eyes –
it belongs in a Palace, not in the Tower

ANE. Never in my apartments. Hvorfor fanden kom vi
overhovedet til England!

She sweeps out.

SUFFOLK. Her Majesty is distressed because someone has
removed all the old Queen's dresses.

JAMES. Och, buy some more – it's the Promised Land.

SUFFOLK *goes.*

Oh, cheer up, Cecil – you look like a beagle I used to have

LENNOX. Mr Biggles?

JAMES. He does, disne? Come on, Es – I'm raging – let's find
some pretty English boys. Look after the doudou, beagle –
Pax!

NORTHUMBERLAND *and* CECIL *are left.*

N'LAND. You wanted a word.

CECIL. Yes – congratulations by the way – Privy Councillor
and Head of the Royal Bodyguard

N'LAND. Everybody's getting something

CECIL. Christ knows how we're going to afford it all – we had to sell Kent to pay for the old Queen's funeral.

N'LAND. Is it meant to shut me up?

CECIL. Not getting paranoid are you, Harry, in your old age?

N'LAND. There was no mention of toleration in the King's speech.

CECIL. It'll come – we're not enforcing the penalties

N'LAND. Forgive me if I don't raise a glass yet.

CECIL. There is something you could do, Harry – if you wanted to speed it along. The Protestant insurgents in Flanders. The ones you trained.

N'LAND. What about them?

CECIL. Causing the Spanish Governor no end of bother apparently

N'LAND. I thought that was the point of them – it was what you asked me to do

CECIL. Well, you certainly seem to have excelled yourself this time

N'LAND. I liked them – which is why I don't intend to go back there and start shooting them – before you ask

CECIL. wouldn't dream of it – though the Governor would appreciate our help

N'LAND. Is he putting it in the Treaty?

CECIL. No – not at the moment anyway

N'LAND. Because it's not going to play well, is it – English troops helping the Spanish to exterminate Protestants.

CECIL. No – it wouldn't play well

N'LAND. Parliament'd be up in arms

CECIL. and toleration would go on the bonfire. You see it is in your interest to help me with this.

N'LAND. What did you have in mind?

CECIL. We need to make it a Catholic thing.

N'LAND. Go on.

CECIL. You talk to the boys – the Wright brothers, Catesby – all the – what do you call them, 'wasted flower of England'

N'LAND. Wasted by England – Jack Wright's the finest swordsman I ever met

CECIL. their choice, Harry – all they ever needed to do was swear allegiance to the Crown above the Pope

N'LAND. you can have a conscience or a career, is that where we've come to?

CECIL. if they form a regiment to aid the Spanish in Flanders – they get both – a career and a conscience – paid to bash the Prots

N'LAND. you're getting shot of them – that's what you're doing

CECIL. We'll never sell toleration to Parliament with men like Mad Jack Wright on the loose – men we had to bang up every time the old Queen sniffled – this way everyone wins

N'LAND. Most especially you. Because we all know who'll get fat on this peace

CECIL. Harry, you can't imagine I am fostering peace to feather my own nest?

N'LAND. I'm saying you stand to gain – as your father and grandfather gained from the dissolution of the old Church

CECIL. And yours didn't? Look – I know there was nothing about toleration in the speech, but we've suspended the fines, Topcliffe's chained to his perch and you can see the results yourself – I've never known so many Papists hopping about – like bunnies on a sunny bank – the King wants to make toleration work, Harry – he really does

N'LAND. And when he's ready to put it into law – you come and talk to me about your insurgents.

NORTHUMBERLAND *goes.* SUFFOLK *is lingering.*

SUFFOLK. He had dinner with the Governor last night.

CECIL. Northumberland?

SUFFOLK. He wanted the Spanish to include toleration in the Treaty negotiations.

CECIL. What is it about this country? Is everyone drunk on bloodshed? Can no one see that peace is good? Peace makes people happy, prosperous, rich? Please tell me the Governor didn't agree?

SUFFOLK. He's soft in the bedroom not in the head.

CECIL. For this relief – So now we need someone else with a foot in both graves

MONTEAGLE and LIZZIE appear, as if they are walking into the lion's den.

How well do you know our new Lord and Lady Monteagle?

SUFFOLK. Not well enough to know how he came to be Lord Monteagle.

CECIL. Then you should definitely invite us all to dinner.

CECIL goes to greet MONTEAGLE, SUFFOLK leads away LIZZIE.

Scene Three

Continuous action. While GARNET and the Catholics celebrate the mass in relative public, we see discrete fragments of CECIL talking to MONTEAGLE. With each phrase of the 'Gloria' we jump forward in the conversation.

GARNET (*sings*). *Gloria in excelsis Deo.*

CHOIR. *Et in terra pax hominibus bonae voluntatis.*

CECIL. Any regrets?

MONTEAGLE. Regrets?

CECIL. About your letter to the King – declaring yourself a born-again Protestant – I mean, nowadays it's almost fashionable to be a Papist.

MONTEAGLE. God's no regarder of fashion, is he, Sir Robert – he shows us the path – we have to follow.

CECIL. Quite – and would that explain your previous unfashionable relationship with the Spanish Governor of Flanders?

CHOIR. *Laudamus te.*

CECIL. Please – I can keep a secret – and as it happens we need someone who's on good terms with the Governor

CHOIR. *Benedicimus te.*

MONTEAGLE. It would be my regiment?

CECIL. Yours to command – a full commission – licence to recruit – raise monies – negotiate terms

CHOIR. *Adoramus te.*

MONTEAGLE. And would the King know?

CECIL. That you plotted against his accession?

MONTEAGLE. About this regiment in Flanders.

CECIL. He will be made aware that you have done the nation extraordinary service – at the appropriate moment.

CHOIR. *Glorificamus te.*

CECIL. My advice is get a good quartermaster – with a good quartermaster it could be very lucrative. You have someone in mind?

MONTEAGLE. Yes – yes there might be somebody.

CHOIR. *Gratias agimus tibi propter magnam gloriam tuam.*

Scene Four

A bed. WINTER. CATESBY.

WINTER. Come with me – sign up

CATESBY. to die for Monty in Flanders

WINTER. Nobody's talking about dying

CATESBY. Lay down our bright beautiful bodies in the mud and one corner of a foreign field shall be forever England

WINTER. Why do you always assume the worst?

CATESBY. to avoid disappointment

WINTER. It's a job and it's in Flanders

CATESBY. Tom's garden of Eden

WINTER. It's another world, Cat – I think it's like England was before – you know, like in a chapel where you see a saint that's escaped the hammer – or that missal of Garnet's – all over in birds and animals and flowers

CATESBY. what's your point, Tom? – Catholics have a better sense of interior decor? You weren't born when they stripped the altars – it's nostalgia – Get over it.

WINTER. My point is England's not my country – I have no life here – a younger son without a prospect of a post or a commission

CATESBY. It's all change, Tom – new dawn – look, Monty's got a peerage – and permission to recruit for Flanders – toleration's right around the corner

WINTER. Do you believe that?

CATESBY. I thought I was the one who assumed the worst – Garnet was right – I was wrong

WINTER. Monty's peerage came from a grovelling letter to James I wrote for him – they're letting him recruit because he sent his bollocks to them in an envelope

CATESBY. and yet you'd follow him to Flanders

WINTER. it's a job

CATESBY. in Flanders

WINTER. it's what I can do to serve the faith

CATESBY. in Flanders

WINTER. I don't know what you're saying

CATESBY. Do you think England's going to hell, Tom? – fair question – are your countrymen dancing down the primrose path?

WINTER. I told you – England's not my country

CATESBY. It's where God planted you – shaped you from the soil of England and blew English air into your mouth – and now you'd sooner feed your body than save your nation's soul.

WINTER. Cat, they wouldn't rise up against the old bitch, they'll never stir against good King Jimmy

CATESBY. No, they won't – you're right – they never will –
they is where we've always been wrong – putting our trust in
them – they will never change anything – only we will – us.

WINTER. Who?

CATESBY. You – me – God – I think it's enough. (*Holds out a
primer.*) If you want to know you'll have to swear.

WINTER. You imagine I'd betray you?

CATESBY. Sorry it's a bit primitive – no birds and flowers. I
swear by Jesus Christ Our Saviour that I shall not reveal
what I am about to hear, on peril of my immortal soul.

WINTER *repeats the oath.*

WINTER. Well?

CATESBY. Look out of the window – what do you see?

WINTER. The river – the Strand – Cecil's garden –
Westminster Palace.

CATESBY. Sometimes I lie here looking at it – I dream in one
instant Parliament bursts like a rotten fruit – spattering
every kind of creeping thing across the sky – sun shrouded
with limbs and heads and tongues.

WINTER. Jesus, Cat, your head.

CATESBY. That's a shilling – blasphemy.

WINTER. I didn't curse.

CATESBY. You can curse all you fucking well like, but I won't
have the Lord's name taken in vain – A shilling.

WINTER *finds one.*

What do you know about gunpowder?

WINTER. Not much.

CATESBY. You'll make a pisspoor soldier of Christ.

WINTER. It's what you put in guns and mines and canons. It's
sulphur and charcoal and saltpetre. You put a flame to it and
it goes bang.

CATESBY. What happens when you drop it?

WINTER. What's this now – the Inquisition?

CATESBY. You're meant to be a quartermaster – I've got a hogshead of gunpowder – I drop it on the floor – am I dead or alive?

WINTER. Alive.

CATESBY. Bravo

WINTER. But it decays

CATESBY. like love? Like flesh?

WINTER. goes brown – then it's useless.

CATESBY. See, you know a lot. How much would you need to blow up Parliament?

WINTER. I – don't know

CATESBY. Go on, Tom – admit the justice of it – it's in Parliament that they've royally buggered us – made us aliens in our own land. So – supposing God shaped it for their destruction – Blown open like a tart's scab. You – me – God.

WINTER. How would we get inside?

CATESBY. I don't know – but God will open the doors to us – if this is what He wants – He's already shown me how I can get the powder – or you can

WINTER. Monteagle's regiment.

CATESBY. Easy enough, wouldn't it – change an address here – a form there – isn't that what you're meant to be doing to give Monty his cut – so – powder for a boat at Gabriel's Wharf arrives at a lodging in Lambeth

WINTER. Have you talked to anyone else?

CATESBY. I've sung it from the rooftops. Jack Wright.

WINTER. Not Francis?

CATESBY. Can't risk it.

WINTER. He's a cousin.

CATESBY. He's Monteagle's brother-in-law. Blood or sacrament – why should I make him choose? We, Tom – not they. I need you – that's all – I need your brain – I need your beautiful head.

WINTER *is about to speak* – CATESBY *places his hand on his mouth.*

Don't decide now – Let Him guide you – When are you
next in Flanders?

WINTER. A month.

CATESBY. Could you take a message? – there's an old school
friend of Jack's serving with the Spanish. You should meet
him – he knows all about powder – His name's Guy
Fawkes.

Scene Five

A Privy Council meeting. CECIL, TOPCLIFFE,
NORTHUMBERLAND, ARCHBISHOP *and others.*

ELLESMERE. It's the Danish Diva I'm worried about. When
Cecil wanted peace to help the silk merchants, did he mean
just to supply the royal wardrobe?

SOMERSET. The old Queen only dressed like a battleship –
the new one costs as much

ELLESMERE. She's planning this Christmas pageant for
Hampton Court – one show – twice last year's whole
entertainments' budget

ARCHBISHOP. And she wants a mausoleum in the Abbey –
guess who for? The blasted Queen of Scots.

TOPCLIFFE. Toleration, Lol, toleration – everyone's talking
about the old whore again

CECIL (*entering*). Everyone will always talk about the Queen
of Scots, Dicky – she was devastatingly beautiful, died in
her prime and fucked like a rabbit – beg pardon, your
Grace.

TOPCLIFFE. You've seen the figures, Cecil – Papists oozing
out of every cranny.

CECIL. Never put too much faith in figures – eh, Harry? Shall
we get down to business?

ARCHBISHOP *opens Bible.*

N'LAND. King not coming?

CECIL. Let's see what we can get through before he does. Lol?

ARCHBISHOP. May the Lord smile upon our deliberations this day.

ELLESMERE. The King.

Everyone puts out their tobacco. JAMES *enters with* LENNOX *and the Dodo.*

JAMES. Morning, morning – sorry I'm late. (*Sniffs the air.*)

CECIL. Your Majesty has been fencing?

JAMES. Och, the armour? – No, I wear it all the time – Never know when you might need it. Find a seat somewhere, Esme. I'm putting Lennox on the Council.

LENNOX. Keep you on the straight and narrow, eh, beagle?

CECIL. We were about to have prayers.

JAMES. Carry on – as you were.

ARCHBISHOP (*reading colourlessly*). 'Exodus Chapter 1 verse 15 moreover the King of Egypt spoke to the Hebrew midwives and said when ye do your office to the women of the Hebrews if it be a son then ye shall kill him but if it be a daughter let her live. But the midwives feared God and did not as the King of Egypt commanded them and preserved alive the men children.

As the ARCHBISHOP *reads,* JAMES *has risen and is looking over his shoulder.*

Then the King said unto them why have ye done thus and the midwives answered because the Hebrew women are not as the women of Egypt, they are lively and are delivered ere the midwife come at them. God therefore prospered the midwives the people multiplied and were / very mighty

JAMES. Outrageous

ARCHBISHOP. Your Majesty?

JAMES *tears the page out of the Bible.*

Your Majesty, this is the Word of God.

JAMES. You support what these midwives did?

ARCHBISHOP. Not slaughtering the Hebrew boys?

JAMES. Och, and then lying to the King about it. When they tell him Hebrew women come to term sooner, it's a lie, isna? Jew, Egyptian, Dane – alus nine months.

LENNOX. Right, boss.

ARCHBISHOP. In the circumstances, the deception / is one
that one might

JAMES. So you'd agree with this – this comment in the margin
– printed by some lick-finger Puritan in Geneva – 'The
midwives' deception is evil, but their disobedience is
lawful'

ARCHBISHOP. The midwives feared God

JAMES. Aye – but did God command them? – No – and the
King did – 'their disobedience is lawful' – printed in plain
English so that any man could read it – Jivvens crivvens,
they're refugees – King says kill Jewish boys – you kill
them.

ARCHBISHOP. What's in the margin is a commentary, the
opinion / of learned

JAMES. I dinna go to the Bible for opinion – I want the Word
of God – and if this is our Swiss pal's opinon, how do I
know he's even *translated* it correctly? I want a new Bible.
A Bible we can trust. A Bible for Britain.

CECIL. And who would pay for that, Your Majesty?

JAMES. Parliament.

CECIL. They'll never agree.

JAMES. They'll have to.

CECIL. Under what law? What law will Parliament pass to tax
itself to pay for a Bible it doesn't want? Because England
has a Bible – it was translated in Geneva granted, and it is
deeply flawed – but it is also deeply loved.

JAMES. So to please Parliament, I must sit in my stall on
Sunday and hear sedition proclaimed as gospel?

CECIL. No – but there's too much dry tinder around – Union,
Spain, toleration, plague

ELLESMERE. two more deaths in Whitechapel

ARCHBISHOP. one in Westminster

JAMES. Westminster?

ARCHBISHOP. a vagrant

CECIL. and Bibles are highly inflammable.

LENNOX. So's Parliament.

CECIL. If we are to give the nation a glorious, flawless, authorised tribute to the intellectual capacities of our King we will need first to remove some of the fuel. Now, nobody's seriously going to argue against peace with Spain –

SOMERSET. on the right terms

CECIL. on the right terms

ELLESMERE. We could find a better name for the Union

JAMES. What's wrong with Britannia?

ELLESMERE. It means the Land of Brute

JAMES. he was the great grandson of Aeneas

SOMERSET. it does sound like we're calling ourselves a nation of savages

LENNOX. which is what you English think the Scots are

CECIL. I think we can say that everyone is in favour of Union in principle – ?

Silence.

The plague we'll do what we've always done – prorogue Parliament, ban gatherings, seal the city

TOPCLIFFE. Which leaves the Papists.

CECIL. Thank you, Dicky.

N'LAND. We can't go back to persecuting Catholics just to pacify the Commons

CECIL. Nobody's begun to mention persecution, Harry

ELLESMERE. but a return to the status quo would help us at the Exchequer. Recusancy Tax was bringing in £3000 a year

N'LAND. It's not a tax – it's a fine

ELLESMERE. We prefer to think of it as tax – we allow them to bunk off Church – they pay us for the privilege. £3000 would, as an example, pay the outstanding costs of the Coronation

JAMES. Och, it had to be big – there were ambassadors and – No. I will no' blush for ma ain Crooning

CECIL. Nobody expects it. However, we must now look at the figures

LENNOX. If there's a million Catholics each paying a shilling a week how come it's only £3000?

CECIL. There isn't a million Catholics

LENNOX. That's no' what I heard

CECIL. There isn't.

JAMES. How many are there?

TOPCLIFFE. Too many

CECIL. By their nature, precise figures are very hard to come by. / In addition to the registered recusants

TOPCLIFFE. I've always said we should make them wear badges – a red badge / would

N'LAND. how about branding them

TOPCLIFFE. that would work / too

CECIL. As I was trying to explain – in addition to the known recusants there are the Church Papists, who go to Church on Sunday and escape the fines, / but harbour Romish sympathies. In addition there are

ARCHBISHOP. Increasing all the time – Durham's reported two / thousand

N'LAND. Durham would – Durham sees Catholics / under every gooseberry bush

TOPCLIFFE. They're like rats / – if you stop putting out traps

N'LAND. They are not rats

TOPCLIFFE. they breed like them / – be a million before you know it

N'LAND. they are loyal subjects of His Majesty

ELLESMERE. who won't swear the oath of allegiance

N'LAND. because it breaks their duty to the Pope – and so to God

SOMERSET. which is why we do not allow them to serve in the army or in the government

LENNOX. Aye – but if there's a million of them – and increasing – shouldn't we be a wee bit concerned?

CECIL. For the last time – there isn't a million Catholics – if there were, every third person round this table would be a Papist and the price of rosaries would be through the roof

LENNOX. Don't get the fecking hump with me

N'LAND. Why, when it's Puritans that preach republicanism, Parliament that flouts the will of the monarch, is it the Catholics we hang for disloyalty?

CECIL. Because, Harry, Parliament has never plotted with alien powers to invade this country and has no alliance to a foreign prince who issued a death sentence on our Queen. It has no priests who run secret schools where young men are indoctrinated in deceit – it does not lie and call it equivocation – it does not murder and call it God's work – it does not espouse a philosophy that legitimises regicide and has never to my knowledge tried to murder a king.

N'LAND. The Catholics of England had great hopes of toleration with the King's coming

JAMES. Aye, when I was told there was a million of them in a land worth millions. Now I don't know how many there are and my coffers are empty. So – what I propose is – we count them up and then make them pay – every one – backdated to the day of my accession – that way we fatten the Exchequer, stop Parliament belly-aching – and I get to have my Bible – yes?

CECIL. If that is your desire, Your Majesty

JAMES. I like it, beagle – I do – it's very British.

The Dodo cries 'Pax'.

Scene Six

NORTHUMBERLAND *steps out of the Privy Council and meets* PERCY. CATESBY *is watching.*

PERCY. He shook this hand – he shook this bloody hand

N'LAND. Listen – if there's anything I can do

PERCY. Monteagle's having a field day at my expense

N'LAND. money

PERCY. says he'll publish a broadside – 'Bugger-All For Rome' to the tune of 'Old Queen's Fancy'

N'LAND. I could get you a commission

PERCY. It's not the money, Harry – though if I have to start bribing justices

N'LAND. I could give you a commission in the Royal Bodyguard tomorrow.

PERCY. I'd have to swear allegiance – I'd have to swear an oath I don't believe – Harry, my pride's in tatters – don't ask me to surrender my conscience as well

N'LAND. then don't swear. Administrative oversight – lost the paperwork. The Royal Bodyguard is a good post – entitles you to digs in Westminster Palace – go anywhere, talk to anyone

PERCY. the King?

N'LAND. You'd be in his household.

NORTHUMBERLAND *goes.*

CATESBY. What'll you do, Perce – whisper toleration in th'imperial ear – or cut his throat?

PERCY. He deserves to die

CATESBY. The King or Cecil?

PERCY. why not both? – they can only hang me once

CATESBY. No, Perce – if you're going to sacrifice your life – do it in a worthwhile cause

JACK *and* KIT WRIGHT *emerge from the shadows.*

Elsewhere, CECIL *meets with* TRESHAM.

CECIL. Francis, I need you to get a message to Garnet. Tell him to get out of the country by Christmas – after that he'll be fair game.

CATESBY. Jack Wright, you know – and Kit, his brother.

TRESHAM. Why now?

CECIL. Because there's a storm coming – and I don't want him in the way – tell him to take his whore – what's her name, Anne Vaux – with him

WINTER *has emerged with* FAWKES.

CATESBY. And Tom Winter.

TRESHAM. Why do you care – why do you care what happens to Garnet?

CECIL. I told you, Francis – there's a storm coming – and he's a fucking lightning conductor.

FAWKES. Guido Fawkes. I think you once tried to shoot me in Antwerp.

Snap change: the stage is left to PERCY, CATESBY, WINTER, FAWKES, JACK *and* KIT.

PERCY. I don't know, Cat – I don't know about this.

CATESBY. What don't you know?

PERCY. Any of it – gunpowder – foreign mercenaries

CATESBY. Fawkes is not a mercenary

JACK. and he's as English as you or me

PERCY. So why are we paying him?

FAWKES. to show your seriousness

PERCY. I don't doubt ours

FAWKES. then what are you sweating about at the moment? To achieve a sacred end, a material sacrifice is required – good Jesuit principle

CATESBY. and unless you want to squat on a ton of gunpowder until Parliament is recalled, you'll need a servant in Westminster

FAWKES. John Johnson – at your service. Guy Fawkes was never here.

JACK. I heard he died in Antwerp, Kit

KIT. Blown apart by his own mine

FAWKES. No, Jack – I blew out of your life ten year ago and you've heard nowt of me since – don't lie if you don't need to. Talk cellars to me, Thomas Percy.

PERCY. It's not a cellar – it's a storeroom next to my lodgings in Westminster Palace Yard. I've told the landlord I'll need it for provisions, firewood – for when the family come to town.

FAWKES. It's above river?

PERCY. It runs on ground level right beneath the Chamber

FAWKES. How much powder can we get?

CATESBY. Three dozen

FAWKES (*laughs*). Three dozen?

CATESBY. We could get more, couldn't we, Tom – if it's not enough?

FAWKES. Enough to make a hole the size of Westminster – if you can get three dozen – get it

WINTER. It will be a massacre of innocents.

CATESBY. It's war now, Tom – they've loosed the dogs on us

WINTER. The King, Cecil, Council – but all Parliament?

KIT. Anyone in Parliament's had his chance to speak

JACK. had his chance and – blown it

WINTER. And those who wait in a robing room – who serve a meal?

FAWKES. They chose this work.

WINTER. Poverty chose it – and cut open the heart of any pauper in London – there'll be an image of the Virgin. If we slaughter them, we're no better than the enemy

CATESBY. And if we stay our hand, they will be tortured – in this life, or endlessly in hell

WINTER. Listen – Cat, maybe you should do this without me

CATESBY. God has brought us this far – do we now turn back

WINTER. I'll get you the powder, / but

CATESBY. The thief is proud he does not murder his victim. You do still believe in hell, don't you, Tom – you know this is not about England, here and now – it is about all time.

WINTER. That's my fear – that we will all go to hell.

PERCY. I'm with Tom – we have no authority

FAWKES. like a King's command?

JACK. We have the authority of injustice

CATESBY. It's not enough, though, is it, Perce? Tom? We need the sanction of the Holy Mother Church. Well, she's coming. Garnet's coming here tonight – it's Christmas Eve – a fine night to bury old differences – we'll ask him.

Scene Seven

The preparation for a pageant. JAMES (*for the first time not wearing armour*), ANE, CECIL.

JAMES. How long does this show go on?

ANE. It's the whole history of Britain.

JAMES. I couldnae just watch your scenes?

ANE. I'm Britannia – I'm on throughout.

JAMES. But you've got twelve costume-changes.

ANE. Britain is a rich and complex character.

CECIL. Complex certainly – I don't know how much longer she'll be rich.

ANE. ?

CECIL. Just noting the opulence.

JAMES. Hey, beagle, stab me.

CECIL. You're not wearing your armour.

ANE. It's about to start.

JAMES. That's the point – stab me

ANE. Go and sit down.

JAMES. Stab me – it's an order

CECIL *does so.*

!

CECIL. Your Majesty

JAMES. Och, fine – just a bit harder than I'd expected. Good, eh?

A PAGEANT MASTER *has come onstage, and is waiting awkwardly.*

You see there are metal plates stitched into the

ANE. Skrid din bøssekarl!

JAMES. OK, OK.

> CECIL *and* JAMES *take their seats. The show begins.*

PAGEANT MASTER. This our argument –

> Two thousand eight hundred and fifty years after this world was shaped from nought; eleven hundred and sixteen before the coming of Our Lord

JAMES (*to* CECIL). Maybe we can slip away at the interval.

CECIL. If there is one.

> *As the* PAGEANT MASTER *introduces the show, we see in dumbshow the arrival of* GARNET *and* ANNE *to the conspirators.* CATESBY *shows obeisance, kneeling to kiss* GARNET'*s hand and then shaking* ANNE'*s.*

PAGEANT MASTER. Sir Brute, fleeing the toppling towers of Troy, came upon these shores of Albion. He slew the monstrous Gogmagog and named the fertile island Britain for himself. By Thames' fair side, he built New Troy and there he dwelt in peace. Till death approached and Brute, knowing not which of his sons to prefer, divided Britannia in three – giving to Camber the West, Albany the North and to Locrin the lion's part.

BRITANNIA (ANE).
> When three possess what one did solely owe
> It makes more ways to harm than many know,
> And so prov'd that division of the land
> It brought in war – that hellish firebrand.

> *A sweep of the stage revealing* GARNET, ANNE VAUX, CATESBY, PERCY, WINTER, JACK, KIT *at the end of dinner.* FAWKES *clearing. A game of 'Ace and Bone' is about to begin. Laughter.*

GARNET (*dealing*). I have no idea where it came from – but that's what it said – 'Secretary Cecil says leave before Christmas or expect storm' – looked like it had crossed half England to find me. What's the stake?

CATESBY. Three avemarias for the bone – one paternoster for thirty-one. So what did you reply ?

GARNET. What is there to reply to a message passed from hand to hand? (*To* ANNE VAUX.) Are you in?

ANNE VAUX. but tomorrow is Christmas and he is still in England – No

CATESBY. and the storm rages

GARNET. We should have a drink, shouldn't we? – to go with the game

PERCY. Johnson

FAWKES *fills glasses. Cards are turned over.*

GARNET. Dealer wins the bone – and twenty-nine. Thank you for this, Robert – it's like the old days – with Anne's father and yours

ANNE VAUX. we shall not see their like again

GARNET. Thomas Tresham is still with us

CATESBY (*raising a glass*). Good Sir Thomas. The last of old England.

ALL. Sir Thomas.

GARNET*'s hands are trembling too much to shuffle the cards.*

ANNE VAUX. Let me.

ANNE VAUX *takes the deck from him and deals.*

CATESBY. Who knows where we shall be next Christmas – pushing up poppies in Flanders

ANNE VAUX. Flanders? Are you leaving?

CATESBY. you've heard of Monteagle's regiment

GARNET. He came and asked me for my blessing

CATESBY. Did you give it?

GARNET. Of course – there's no stricture against fighting in a just cause

CATESBY. and this is just

GARNET. We're at peace with Spain – he's defending the faith – I see no obstacle – Jack takes the bone and

KIT. Thirty

GARNET. So I'm down for three avemarias and a paternoster – are we keeping our own tabs?

JACK *is dealing.*

CATESBY. Because this is important, Henry – we've all been asked to join this regiment – not Percy but the rest – we will be going to Flanders to fight, to kill – maybe to die

ANNE VAUX. when? – I mean, when do you leave?

CATESBY. As soon as the King calls a parliament

WINTER. plague permitting

CATESBY. So we need to know – is it just – is it lawful?

ANNE VAUX. He's told you – he gave Monteagle his blessing

CATESBY. Please, Anne – we need to hear from Henry – supposing the insurgents have taken hold of a town – a garrison – no, a town – they're holding it against us – is it lawful for us to destroy it?

GARNET. Of course – If you're defending your common-wealth – in this case the faith – it's natural law and no authority could deny you – a commonwealth must be able to protect and provide for itself – or it's unworthy of the name – (*Of the game.*) mine again

ANNE VAUX. and mankind's worse than beasts

GARNET. who have both the means and instinct to defend themselves

WINTER. But we're not beasts – We live by God's command-ment – 'Thou shalt not kill'

GARNET. But surely He could not have meant His commandment to leave us defenceless, Tom? – when the common good is at risk we must say the soldier under orders does not kill, any more than the public executioner – he is a sword of justice for the common good

CATESBY. Yet suppose the situation's this – this town the insurgents occupy – which I must seize, for from it they inflict untold cruelty upon the commonwealth – our commonwealth – the faith – this town is full of civilians – non-combatants – women, children – suppose I cannot take this town without I inflict enormous casualties?

WINTER. Do we say to these innocents – we prefer our common good to yours?

ANNE VAUX. The child of an enemy is not an innocent, the wife of an enemy is not an innocent

GARNET. No, Tom's right to doubt – the death of a criminal is a boon to the commonwealth – the death of an innocent can never be.

CATESBY. Then all wars are unlawful – and Percy at least amongst us is a murderer and will go to hell – am I right? – never in history has an army taken a city without killing a civilian

GARNET. And the Church fathers long since accepted this – innocents will be killed – their deaths – unintentional – may be unavoidable – even necessary – and then they are lawful.

Silence.

Imagine I'd been shot with a poisoned bullet here – my arm is poisoned – if I don't cut it off I will die. My hand – my fingers – they're unharmed – but if I cut off the arm – which I must do in order to live – then the fingers and hand will go into the fire with it – per accidens. These innocents too, whose deaths no one intends, may die – but per accidens – a side effect.

CATESBY. So, if the cause is just – if there is no way to take the citadel – to defend our commonwealth – but to blow all to pieces, that is what we must do?

GARNET. We cannot truly know God until we have laid all else aside – our pride, our vanity

PERCY. Our conscience?

GARNET. Our conscience too may be vanity – until we are ready to sacrifice all mortal things – we shall not be worthy of His love.

A church bell begins to ring.

ANNE VAUX. We should go.

CATESBY. Stay – you can lead mass here – for Christ's soldiers soon to leave these shores.

GARNET. Anne – will you help me?

CATESBY. Through here.

CATESBY *shows* ANNE VAUX *and* GARNET *to another room and then comes back. He takes out his primer. They lay their hands upon it.*

I swear by the blessed Trinity, and by the holy sacrament I now purpose to receive never to disclose by word or circumstance this work of God's will – nor shall I desist from the execution of it, until the rest shall give me leave.

GARNET *re-appears in vestments. He carries a covered chalice.*

GARNET. In nomine Patris, et Filii, et Spiritus Sancti. Amen. *Introibo ad altare Dei.*

ALL. *Ad deum qui laetificat*

GARNET. *Judica me Deus, et discerne causam meam de gente non sancta: ab homine iniquo et doloso erue me*

The pageant climax sweeps across the stage, drowning out GARNET. BRITANNIA (ANE) *is between flags of St Andrew and St George.*

BRITANNIA.
All hail that second Brute, James our King!
Whose name did to us heav'nly comfort bring;
When in despair our hopes lay drooping dead,
And comfort from men's hearts was gone and fled,
He set his wreath of Union
Upon the head of Albion
So let trumpet's silver sing this lay:
God save King James – O! 'Tis a happy day!

As the conspirators take communion, Union flags fly down.

ACT THREE

Scene One

A hand bell tolls.

CANTOR. *Dirige, Domine, Deus meus, in conspectu tuo viam meam.*

Red crosses are marked on the doors of the city. Figures move around in plague masks like large birds. Under FAWKES' *direction, barrels are rolled into the cellar.*

Scene Two

The bay of a hound – PERCY *chasing* EDWARD. *A garden.*

PERCY. The otter is lithe – but the pack is swifter – the otter darts – makes one bolt for his holt – and the pack gobbles him up.

They tumble to the ground laughing. MARTHA *and* LIZZIE *come by –* LIZZIE *is dressed in black.*

MARTHA. Perce – William and Lizzie are leaving – Where's Henry?

EDWARD. Asleep

ANNE VAUX (*entering*). He's sleeping, Martha – do you want me to wake him?

LIZZIE. No – let him rest. I wanted to say goodbye

ANNE VAUX. To be honest I don't know if I could – he's as fast as a child – these days on the road

LIZZIE. Where do you stop next?

ANNE VAUX. The Digbys – Everard is riding over to meet us – and then into Wales

LIZZIE. I wish I could have joined you – I've never been to Holywell – But William says now's not the time to be seen on a pilgrimage, even one masked as a hunting party – and I don't like to leave Francis for long

ANNE VAUX. How is he?

LIZZIE. Like a ghost – he wouldn't leave the bedside – all six nights while Father writhed and shivered – when the end came and Christ took him to rest – I thought Francis would find some peace too – but he sits by the empty bed staring – as if into some endless and terrifying future

ANNE VAUX. He's lost his father, Lizzie – now he has no choice but to be a man – that's frightening. Robert was the same.

PERCY *chases* EDWARD *off again – baying.*

MARTHA. I don't know – some men manage not to grow up, however long their fathers have been gone.

ANNE VAUX. Is something troubling you, Martha?

MARTHA. No – only having my home turned into a boarding house – not you, Anne – but these men who appear at dusk and leave in the morning – it used to be our enemies who kept me awake – now it's our friends.

ANNE VAUX. It's been the same ever since we left London – I asked Henry – he told me not to worry – that it was all to do with

MARTHA. Flanders

ANNE VAUX. The sooner they sail, the better

MONTEAGLE, PERCY, EDWARD *and* WINTER *arrive.*

MONTEAGLE. We should leave if we're going to get you to Francis before nightfall. Martha – it's been a joy – quite like the old days – loved to have stayed longer – but the King commands – silly old ponce – you should hear the things they say about him, eh, Perce?

CATESBY *has entered from another direction.*

CATESBY. What do they say about him, Monty?

MONTEAGLE. Robert – good to see you – off, I'm afraid

CATESBY. What do they say about the King, Monty?

MONTEAGLE. Oh – y'know – the usual – Give our best to
Henry, Anne – I hope St Winifrid works her magic – it's the
miracle we're all gunning for – Come along everybody.

WINTER. I need a word with Cat – I'll catch you on the road.

They pass through – leaving CATESBY *and* WINTER.

I thought you wouldn't get here

CATESBY. Jack was delayed at John Grant's. Who have you
spoken to?

WINTER. Keyes and Rookwood.

CATESBY. Your brother?

WINTER. We came there two days after the constables had
stolen his sheep and torched his barn – they're our best
recruiting sergeants – after Garnet.

PERCY *returns.*

At every house they ask how can God permit this? And
Henry replies because we have not striven hard enough –
it's as if he wants us to succeed

PERCY. He's growing suspicious

CATESBY. I know that, Perce – why do you think I'm here? –
has he said why he's taken to the road?

WINTER. Because there's nowhere he can risk more than a
night or two

PERCY. He's going to Holywell – to the shrine – Anne wants
him to bathe in the water – he wants to give strength to the
faithful

WINTER. I want to talk to Francis

CATESBY. No

WINTER. We need money, Cat – and we'll go on needing it
until Parliament is called – Francis inherited half
Cambridgeshire

CATESBY. Francis then – and no more.

WINTER. Thirteen – it's not enough

CATESBY. We, Tom – not they – when the time comes – these
thirteen will achieve more than an army of infidels.

WINTER. I should go. (*They kiss.*) I'll see you in Wales.

WINTER *goes*.

CATESBY. Cheer up – Perce – it might not happen. Where's Garnet?

PERCY. Inside

CATESBY. I want to see him while Anne's away

PERCY. He's asleep – the sleep of the just.

CATESBY. Smile, Percy

PERCY. We've deceived him – we are deceiving him – God's voice in this land

CATESBY. We equivocated, Perce – we told a lie to protect the faith – and what kind of a lie? Don't they threaten your livelihood, your commonwealth – your beautiful wife and fine son? Be easy – I'll talk to him – the path will be made clear.

PERCY. It's not only Garnet who's suspicious

CATESBY. Then spin her some tale, Percy – tell her you've got a mistress – tell her you're in debt – tell her you're in love with me – women gossip – you tell Martha – she'll tell Lizzie who'll tell Monty – or she'll tell Anne – either will hang us.

He goes. MARTHA *returns.*

PERCY. Where's Edward?

MARTHA. He wanted to show Anne the new horses.

Beat.

PERCY. I think I may just go and lie down before dinner

MARTHA. Are you sick?

PERCY. Tired

MARTHA. You hardly slept at all last night

PERCY. It's the heat – did I disturb you? – you know I never sleep well in summer

MARTHA. And at supper – when you suddenly arose – walked about – musing – and sighing – with your arms across – and when I asked you what the matter was – stared at me

PERCY. I told you – it's the weather

MARTHA. Which will not let you eat – or sleep – or talk – except to these men who gather in huddles by our hearth

PERCY. What men? – Tom, Robert – Jack – you know them

MARTHA. I used to – but now they hide their eyes when I come near – or like you, stare through me – I'm your wife, Thomas Percy, and by the beauty you once commended – by all your vows of love and that great vow which made us one – unfold to me – yourself – your half

PERCY. Martha – please

MARTHA. Within the bond of marriage should I know no secrets – I am yourself but to keep at meals – talk to you – comfort your bed – am I your harlot?

PERCY. You are my true and honourable wife – as dear to me as

MARTHA. If this is true, then I should know your cause of grief

PERCY. There's none

MARTHA. Granted I'm a woman – and so by definition unable to keep counsel – but look – (*She cuts herself.*) I bleed like a man

PERCY. O God – Martha – no, stop this – stop it

CATESBY *steps in.*

CATESBY. Is somebody hurt?

PERCY. She fell down – there must have been some glass

CATESBY. Here, let me. (*He binds it with his handkerchief.*) That's a nasty cut – it must have hurt – You are a valiant woman, Martha Percy – and discretion is the better part of valour – Perce is fortunate to have such a resourceful helpmeet.

GARNET, *looking more frail, enters. He wears everyday clothes.*

GARNET. I heard voices

PERCY. It's nothing, Father – an accident

GARNET. Where are the others?

PERCY. They've gone

GARNET. Why did no one wake me?

MARTHA. Anne told us not to disturb you

GARNET. I had a present for – Is that Robert?

CATESBY. Yes, Father

He kisses GARNET*'s hand.*

GARNET. Is there any wine, Martha – my throat

MARTHA. I'll find you some

She goes.

GARNET. I'm sorry I missed them – I had something for Francis

PERCY. I'm just going to – um – see if – a hand

CATESBY. Percy (*Puts his finger to his lips.*)

PERCY *goes.*

I got your letter.

GARNET. You were lucky to find us – never anywhere more than a day or two – or even the same identity – it's a strange feeling – like moving across England in a forest of names.

CATESBY. You must be used to it by now

GARNET. Yes – I suppose I must.

CATESBY. You're going to St Winifrid's.

GARNET. It's a journey I have long meant to make.

ANNE VAUX *returns with a bottle of wine and a glass.*

ANNE VAUX. Martha said you wanted something to drink.

GARNET. Robert's here.

ANNE VAUX. I know – do you feel better?

GARNET. Ready for the road again – I worry about Anne, Robert – in another age – in another land – she would rule over a convent – teach and guide the generations – instead of being handmaiden to an invalid

ANNE VAUX. Our Lady called herself handmaid

GARNET. The Lord's – not to some – what did you call me once, Robert – fop. How's Flanders? – each day I expect to be summoned to the docks – I say to Anne, 'Today will be the day' – 'we could take a picnic'

CATESBY. We cannot sail until Parliament is recalled

GARNET. Yes – yes – Monty explained it all

CATESBY. He did.

GARNET. Monty has no doubts about Flanders.

CATESBY. Henry – if you want to talk to me

ANNE VAUX. Oh, don't mind me – the handmaid knows her place.

She goes. Silence.

GARNET. So – what do you have to say to me?

CATESBY. You wrote to me.

GARNET. But I assume by your presence that you have something to say – and before you speak, you should know that I've written to Rome – I've told them what I've heard and what I've seen

CATESBY. Which is?

GARNET. Sheaves of swords and muskets – fine horses – whispering in every gallery – conversations that break off when I come near

CATESBY. And what has Rome replied?

GARNET. I am forbidden to meddle in any stir against the Crown – instructed to shun the company of all who seek to engage me – even in order to hinder them – but should any direct evidence – or names – reach me, I am at liberty to pass it to the government.

Silence.

CATESBY. Do you believe in God, Henry?

GARNET. You know the answer.

CATESBY. 'Whosoever shall say unto this mountain, Be thou removed, and shall not doubt in his heart, it shall come to pass.' Could you remove a mountain?

GARNET. If God instructed me.

CATESBY. That's God doing it himself. Could you do it – because of your belief in God?

GARNET. Perhaps.

CATESBY. But you're not sure.

GARNET. My belief may not be perfect.

CATESBY. 'The Son of Man said "I know thy works, thou art neither cold nor hot, so then because thou art lukewarm I will spue thee out of my mouth."' Frightening words.

GARNET. The Book of the Apocalypse contains great terror and great beauty.

CATESBY. I love you, Father.

GARNET. And I you, Robert – but is this what you rode here to tell me?

CATESBY. No.

Beat.

GARNET. It is surprising that the Lamb loves the cold better than the lukewarm, isn't it. You do not wish to be lukewarm.

CATESBY. If you are forbidden to meddle – why did you write to me?

GARNET. Because I believe you must be in torment – and it would be the greater sin to abandon you.

CATESBY. But I may not speak to you. I have sworn a vow – a sacramental oath – my lips are sealed.

GARNET. You may confess to me.

CATESBY. I may?

GARNET. Confession is no breach of an oath.

CATESBY. You want me to – you would hear my confession?

GARNET. I cannot deny it.

CATESBY *kneels.*

Dominus sit in corde tuo et labiis tuis ut rite et perfecte confitearis omnia peccata tua. In nomine Patris, Filio et Spirito Sancto. Amen.

CATESBY. Amen. There are three dozen barrels of gunpowder in the vaults beneath Parliament. They're loaded down with pig iron, ballast, nails. On the day when the King comes to open Parliament – when they array themselves in their ermine and scarlet to devise new instruments of torment for the faithful – we shall blow them all to hell.

A silence.

GARNET. This is a mortal sin, Robert

CATESBY. We are in no rebellion against God – we are defending His Truth – against those who have sinned against the Holy Spirit.

GARNET. Vengeance is God's not ours

CATESBY. But we are God's hands – how is His vengeance to be exacted?

GARNET. Then if you are so sure there is no sin – why your distress – why the need for confession?

CATESBY. As a knight going into battle – to purify our deeds – from anger, envy, pride – it must be a blow struck cold

GARNET. I cannot absolve you of murder – of an act of monstrous vanity which will bring disaster upon the Church

CATESBY. A greater vanity than the martyr's? Whose innocence and courage in the face of death bears witness to God's power and presence in the world – so shall these innocents and our courage bear witness to the might and magnificence of the Lord – If the death of one innocent is glorious, how much greater the death of hundreds?

GARNET. Robert, this is not even chopped logic – it is bestiality – where is the courage in gunpowder?

CATESBY. So if we went at them with an axe or a halberd it would be allowable?

GARNET. In your heart you know this is evil

CATESBY. In my heart I love God – in my heart I am in love with God – hopelessly, besottedly, idolatrously even – for His love I would walk through fire and bear a thousand wounds – The love you inflamed – I am your creation, Henry – we all are.

GARNET. Then I must ask forgiveness of you.

CATESBY. What cause? – Your failure to live the belief you taught? – The path is narrow and few walk there – Live it in us – The sons of your word.

GARNET. I have nurtured a brood of serpents – infected you with my pride. O God, is this what you have preserved me for? To bear me through the terror and pestilence for this? Robert, you cannot do this – You have no authority.

CATESBY. We have the authority of our souls

GARNET. which are in the possession of hell

CATESBY. Do you believe that? Do you believe this is the devil's work?

GARNET. The Church has always shown herself more glorious by enduring than by fighting

CATESBY. The Church has shown herself most glorious when she has ridden with Our Saviour against the armies of the beast

GARNET. The Pope has forbidden any commotion

CATESBY. He has forbidden you to meddle with it – to hinder it – and I am not bound to take knowledge of the Pope's will from you – who denied his flock before – Why did you ever show me that Brief if this is not what you wanted to happen? – if you so love peace why did you not leave when Cecil gave you the chance?

GARNET. Because I would not abandon the flock to the wolves

CATESBY. and because you love God more than you love peace. I have made my confession – will you not absolve me?

GARNET. I cannot.

CATESBY. Why not?

GARNET. Because there is neither humility nor reason within you.

CATESBY. Was Christ humble when he drove the sinners from the Temple – reasonable when he told his disciples to hate their father and mother if they were to follow him?

GARNET. And if I go now – to the government and tell them this?

CATESBY. You will have broken the seal of the sacrament – you will have set the King and the powers of this world before God – and He will spue you out of his mouth.

GARNET. I don't know which to fear more – your success or your failure.

CATESBY. Then pray for us.

CECIL appears in his garden.

Pray for us – and I will allow you this condition – if you are caught before we triumph – or we miss – and you are threatened with torture – if you are tortured – then you may break this seal

GARNET. Why this condition?

CATESBY. Because I'm not cruel – and because if you had no choice, you would be a victim – and not a martyr.

He goes. GARNET sinks down.

KATHERINE SUFFOLK comes to CECIL. In CECIL's garden, it is nearly dawn.

SUFFOLK. Come to bed

CECIL. I can't sleep.

SUFFOLK. What is it?

CECIL. My back – my legs – my head

SUFFOLK. Let me

She massages his back. ANNE VAUX comes to GARNET.

ANNE VAUX. What did he say?

CECIL. Look at the tulips

ANNE VAUX. What did he say?

CECIL. like an army of imams in their turbans.

SUFFOLK. Ghosts in the twilight.

CECIL. I love them for their patience.

GARNET. Too long, Anne

CECIL. Fists of life bunched in the earth all winter waiting for the sun to call them.

GARNET. Too long – we have lurked in the darkness

He goes.

CECIL. I have the Spanish Governor hanging around in Dover to sign a Peace Treaty – but the King won't recall Parliament

His back is agony.

SUFFOLK. I'm sorry – I'm sorry

CECIL. No – no – hurts no more than walking – He won't recall Parliament because he's too busy hunting – and terrified of the plague – and hates Parliament because Parliament won't give him any money because Parliament doesn't like the Union

Another stab of pain.

SUFFOLK. What would you give to be free of it?

CECIL. Nothing. My mother paid twenty angels to a surgeon who strapped me to a bench until I screamed – It is my cross – I bear it – And at this precise moment – when the country is on its knees – Garnet goes on a pilgrimage. Why?

GARNET *returns to* ANNE VAUX *with white garments and a bundle. He begins to dress.*

SUFFOLK. They say he suffers from a palsy.

CECIL. You're not serious – you think he's after a miracle?

SUFFOLK. St Winifrid has brought comfort to many who have believed

CECIL. What? – that a pagan prince lopped off a virgin's head and where it landed, a spring leapt from the rock

SUFFOLK. it is a sacred place

CECIL. that a monk put her head back on and she lived to be ninety – I'm asking you – is this what one has to believe – you think that's possible?

SUFFOLK. I've met people who have been cured there

CECIL. you do – don't you – you think it's possible

SUFFOLK. It is a sacred place

CECIL. And if I believed – if I crawled on my hands and knees – plunged my crooked limbs in the living waters of St Winifrid – God would straighten them? Is that what you believe too?

GARNET. If Catesby wishes to turn a pilgrimage into a crusade – then so be it.

SUFFOLK. Wouldn't you want it?

CECIL. Would you love me more?

SUFFOLK. I'm not going to answer that.

CECIL. No – not if my back were straight, my limbs unbound
– but if I believed it could happen – if I believed the miracle
were possible – then you would love me more. True?

SUFFOLK. I pray for your pain to be eased.

CECIL. To whose God? Mine or Garnet's?

SUFFOLK. I told you our first morning together – I will die a
Catholic – as I was born one

CECIL. and this space between – while you are fleshed – what
are you? I watch you beside me sleeping – the two moons
of your eyelids, the whisper of your breath – I think who is
this body? What is the engine of her soul?

SUFFOLK. And what did you divine?

CECIL. I cannot know, can I? – and if I cannot know it of you
– my Countess – opened in ecstasy beneath me, how can
I of anyone? The country is turning feral – We've no King,
no Parliament, no Law, no money – though that doesn't stop
the Queen your mistress spending cash like a sow pisses –
eclipses of the sun and moon – the almanacs prophesy
disaster / and what's its name anyway – this country we're
living in? Nobody knows.

SUFFOLK. I thought you didn't read them – I thought you
didn't read almanacs

CECIL. I don't believe them – but I read them like every other
superstitious sod in this poor, nameless, lawless land – and
who are you? The bitch who tells me to pray for a miracle –
we don't need a miracle – we need a government. Get out
of my garden. Go.

She goes.

And if it's true – if there are a million Catholics – in their
bones, in their heart, in their bowels – living quietly,
minding their business – but always wishing. Lip service on
a Sunday – but inside where I cannot reach – dreaming of
wine that is blood, bread that is flesh, a virgin born of a
virgin born of a virgin – one million of our people in thrall
to an ancient, ungovernable lust for sacrifice – And what if

someone found the way to stir you into action – a flag – a sign to wake you from your slumber – how would one halt that wave?

GARNET *unwraps the bundle: a crucifix.*

ANNE VAUX. And if Cecil comes for you?

GARNET. Then I can play no further part upon Catesby's stage.

Scene Three

CHOIR. *Sanctus!*

CECIL *watches as the crowd of white figures gather beside the sacred pool at St Winifrid's Well. Led by* GARNET *they bathe in the waters.*

ANNE VAUX. We walked up the hill barefoot – the silhouette of the cross before us.

CHOIR. *Sanctus!*

ANNE VAUX. The earth was wet and warm – staining the hem of our garments till we were calf-deep in her must.

CHOIR. *Sanctus!*

ANNE VAUX. The land welcoming us as her own.

CHOIR. *Dominus Deus Sabaoth! Pleni sunt coeli et terra gloria tua.*

ANNE VAUX. At the well's edge Henry took the lead – wading forward into the water – so clear you could see the stones flecked with the virgin's blood – and cold – like ice clasping at your ankles – your knees – your thighs – your belly – and then the overflow of warmth from within – rolling out – as if all your blood had turned to fire – Show yourself!

CHOIR. *Hosanna in excelsis!*

Scene Four

The hunt crashes in on CECIL, *pursuing him as if he were a boar.* JAMES *calls a halt. He is dressed in green. Members of the Privy Council are there – including* NORTHUMBERLAND *– and* QUEEN ANE.

JAMES. Hold! Enough. Have they hurt you, beagle?

CECIL. All major limbs accounted for.

JAMES. You should know better than to go for a stroll in the middle of a boar hunt

CECIL. Your Majesty, / we must speak.

JAMES. Guess who I am – A clue – we're in Sherwood Forest

CECIL. Your Majesty – I regret interrupting your leisure, but we do have to talk

JAMES. Y'know you do look a bit like a boar

LENNOX. mebbe it's the hump

ANE. and the bristly nose

JAMES. and the fangs. Och go on then.

CECIL. You must come back to London.

ANE. Nej.

CECIL. You must come back to London and recall Parliament.

JAMES. I shall be happy if I never set foot again in that plague-ridden pandemonium. What are you trying to do – kill me? (*Sneezes.*)

CECIL. Your Majesty

JAMES. It's nothing – a cold

ANE. ever since he came to fordømte England

CECIL. The people earnestly wish to see their King

JAMES. Wrong, beagle, wrong – the less they see of me, the happier they are – and the feeling's mutual. Es – the note. A billet-doux tied to the collar of ma best hound.

LENNOX (*reading*). 'Dear Mr Jowler

JAMES. that's the name of the beast

LENNOX. please ask His Majesty (because unlike us, he hears you every day) to go back to London. We cannot afford to entertain him any longer.'

JAMES. Naebiddy wants me – naebiddy wants Union – naebiddy wants ma Bible – and me – I'm happy here – under the trees – King of oaks and arbours – so give me ane guid ground for calling Parliament?

CECIL. The Crown's bankrupt. You need to ask for a subsidy.

JAMES. Go cap and knee to a pit of thieves and slackards whose supposed right to govern comes from election by their own slathful and thiefy kindred?

CECIL. We can of course continue to sell off the Crown estates. A forest like this one might fetch / a good price

JAMES. I'm no selling any more land – I'm King o' England, I have to own a bit of it

CECIL. or we could curb the expenses of the Royal Household.

A glance from ANE.

JAMES. Jivvens Crivvens, man – we're not some barren old stick with a few frocks and an orange wig – we've got a family – heirs to the throne – We're no' producing these bairns for our ain pleasure, do ye ken? If the people want a royal family they better pay for it.

CECIL. Of course, Your Majesty – and we can tell them this – but only if you recall Parliament.

JAMES. We should grow mulberry trees.

CECIL. Your Majesty?

JAMES. Britain should become self-sufficient in silk. Imagine this was a forest of mulberries – how many little silkworms there might be – chomping away with their delicate little mandibles. Spinning out their cocoons of finest Nottinghamshire thread.

CECIL. It takes three to five years to mature a mulberry tree and in the meantime

JAMES. you're growing rich on the duty paid by the silk traders. Och I'm no' a fool, Mr Secretary – or leastways I'm wise to you. Harry and I have been talking – I ken that when we sell the Crown estates it's you that buys them –

I ken that the person who'll profit most from peace with Spain is you

CECIL. if His Majesty has any complaint about my conduct, he can dismiss me in the instant

JAMES *seems tempted.* TOPCLIFFE *appears.*

JAMES. Tricky – you found us – lost the prey – caught beagle.

TOPCLIFFE. A hundred Papists have gathered on a hillside in Wales – at St Winifrid's Well – Garnet's there – and we have reports of Robert Catesby – Thomas Winter – Robert Winter – Jack Wright – Kit Wright – half a dozen more with records as long as your arm

JAMES. Where's Wales?

CECIL. Your Majesty is in no imminent danger

JAMES. How fecking far is it to Wales?

CECIL. Your Majesty is in no imminent danger – but you would be safer back in London

JAMES. Go on then, beagle – call your Parliament – summer's nearly over anyway – pick a Tuesday – any Tuesday – nice things always happen to me on Tuesdays

They go leaving CECIL *and* TOPCLIFFE.

CECIL. Nothing, Dicky – do nothing. Put the sheriffs on stand-by – but do nothing – let Garnet make the first move.

Scene Five

GARNET *arrayed in white before the crucifix – he seems recovered.*

GARNET. 'And seeing the multitudes, Christ went up into a mountain, and opening his mouth he taught them, saying: Blessed are the poor in spirit: for theirs is the Kingdom of Heaven' – Not the vaunting spirit, the proud, the puffed up – let them seek the kingdoms of the earth, which shall not last. 'Blessed are the meek – who yield, who do not resist, but overcome evil with good – they shall possess the land. Blessed are they that mourn: for they shall be comforted. Blessed are they that hunger and thirst after justice: for they shall have their fill. Blessed are the merciful: for they shall obtain mercy. Blessed are the clean of heart: they shall see God.' – For we see God in our heart – And as we see light only if our eyes are clear, so we see God only if the heart is clear in its single-mindedness and simplicity of purpose. 'Blessed are the peacemakers for they shall be called the children of God' – because there is nothing in them which stands against God, their father – They have peace within themselves – they have set the passions of their souls in order and so made of themselves a little kingdom of God, where reason holds sway over the beast, and is subject to Truth, the Only Begotten Son – For none may govern unless he is subject to higher powers. From this kingdom of peace, the prince of this world is cast out and though he shall stir from without, he shall only make more manifest the strength of what has been built – And therefore, 'Blessed are they that are persecuted for righteousness' sake, for theirs is the Kingdom of Heaven.'

CHOIR. *Benedictus qui venit in nomine Domine. Hosanna in excelsis!*

GARNET (*over*). And here Our Lord speaks directly to those who were present on the mountain top saying, 'Blessed are ye when they shall revile you, and persecute you, and speak all that is evil against you, untruly, for my sake: Be glad and rejoice for your reward is very great in heaven. For so they persecuted the prophets that were before you.' You fear to lose the silver you gained with great labour, the silver you must leave behind at your death – would you achieve everlasting life without effort? For what could be more fortunately bestowed by God upon any man, than amongst the very butchers, to confess His Name? – The body racked, tortured and quartered, with a dying and a free spirit to confess Christ? – Than to forsake this world and go to heaven? – To leave men and stand amongst angels? By dying to have subdued death which is so feared of all men and by death to have gotten immortality? To enter into the New Jerusalem – where there shall be no more death, where mourning and crying and pain are no more – lit by the splendour of God which is brighter than the sun – A throne at that sacred banquet where Christ himself shall wash away our tears. Does the work terrify you? Then see the reward.

Scene Six

A table of thirteen men. CATESBY *at the centre.*

CATESBY. We have our date, gentlemen. The fifth of November. As the King and Queen are enthroned, Fawkes will light the fuse. From then we have half an hour. Francis will be on the Embankment with the boat waiting to take Fawkes to the docks – then you will ride to the Tower to meet me. The mine goes up – that's King, Queen, Prince Henry

PERCY. In the Savoy, I hear the blast and slit Prince Charlie's throat

CATESBY. Tom and Rookwood start towards Warwick

WINTER. We're in Highgate – how do we know?

FAWKES. they'll hear her blow in Enfield – ash on Gravesend – clouds slick with the grease

CATESBY. There are fresh mounts every thirty miles along the route – at each house let them hear the news, but not your part in it – for the moment confusion is our ally. At two o'clock when rumour swirls throughout the city, Percy and I will make the first proclamation from the Tower

PERCY. If they haven't torn us Papist limb from limb.

CATESBY. We don't mention Rome, Perce – we don't even mention God – we talk about England – and the thieving, filthy, verminous Scots who carve up our pastures – devour our green forests – pollute our mountains and our rivers – who've turned this sceptred isle into a playground for their profit.

At the same hour Jack, Kit, Everard and Robert Winter seize Princess Elizabeth in Warwick and ride for Holbeach, while Grant, Keyes and Bates announce to Catholic houses the fall of the King and the accession of a new Queen loyal to Rome. Once the city is safe we'll send for you to bring the Princess for her coronation.

TRESHAM. And our friends in Parliament – how are they warned?

CATESBY. No one is to be warned

TRESHAM. There are good Catholics in Parliament – who
will flock to our side when the King is dead

CATESBY. If they were good Catholics they would not have
waited – if they were good Catholics they would not be in a
Parliament which has hounded and harried us until we have
no remedy but the sharpest

TRESHAM. Monteagle is my brother-in-law

CATESBY. Northumberland is Perce's cousin – and if my own
son were in that Chamber on November the fifth I would
rather he died than our secret came to light.

TRESHAM. I want no part of this

CATESBY. Fawkes.

FAWKES *steps in* TRESHAM's *way.*

You've sworn a sacred oath, Sir Francis – break it and
there's no way but hell. Why does one man die of plague
and another survive – one killed by an earthquake and
another walks free – let God pick the righteous from the
rubble – we are the instruments of His justice. You never
know, Monty might even get purgatory. Do what you must.
(*Kisses him.*) Gentlemen, to your posts – the next time we
meet will be in a new England – or in paradise.

ACT FOUR

Scene One

Continuous from the end of the previous scene. TRESHAM *is left –* LIZZIE *is now with him.*

LIZZIE. Why? How? Tell me, brother – make sense of it for me.

TRESHAM. Tom came to me – in the days after Father – when I had prayed to God – when I had said – let me not suffer as he did – let me die on the gallows sooner – and there was Tom – and there is something else you must know – for three years I've been Cecil's spy – nothing serious – who's talking to whom – about what – gossip mainly – but it would never end – I knew it would never end – and this – I saw Cecil dead – I saw Cecil's smile smeared across the Thames

LIZZIE. You have made me the one thing I never thought to be – you have made me glad our father is dead. You fool – you stupid – spineless – I hope Cecil made it worth your while – well – did he?

TRESHAM. I haven't been given a peerage, if that's what you mean

LIZZIE. If you think for one moment there is any comparison between William and what you have done (*She hits him.*)

So, Francis – what are you going to do now?

TRESHAM. If they know I have warned William they will kill me – if the plot is exposed, Cecil will send me to the gallows – I don't want to die

LIZZIE. Then pray – ask God to find a way out.

MONTEAGLE *comes to* LIZZIE.

MONTEAGLE. I will kill him – I will rip him apart with my bare hands – and then Tom Winter

LIZZIE. He is trying to save your life

MONTEAGLE. and make me accessory to treason and mass murder

LIZZIE. I don't want Francis to die.

MONTEAGLE. I wish he'd never been born.

LIZZIE. William, if you tell Cecil how you learnt of this, you are murdering my brother

MONTEAGLE. And if I don't – It's my regiment, angel, it's my seal on the fucking dockets – where the fuck is Winter – where the fuck is that little runt

LIZZIE. I've sent for him

MONTEAGLE. when I've finished with him there'll be nothing left to quarter

LIZZIE. You can't touch Tom Winter.

MONTEAGLE. Why – because he's your cousin? He's ready enough to blow me to pieces

LIZZIE. because he is the only way we have of stopping this

CECIL *comes to* MONTEAGLE, *reading a letter.*

CECIL. 'My lord – Out of the love I bear to you I have a care for your preservation. Therefore I advise you, as you tender your life, to devise some excuse to shift off your attendance at this Parliament. For God and man hath concurred to punish the wickedness of this time. Think not slightly of this advice – for though there be no appearance of any stir – they shall receive a terrible blow this Parliament and yet they shall not see who hurts them.'

It's unsigned.

MONTEAGLE. It was handed to me in the street by a stranger. A tall man.

CECIL. 'Out of the love I bear to you . . . '

MONTEAGLE. Could be anybody. I didn't recognise the handwriting.

CECIL. You wouldn't – it's been disguised – is it a hoax?

MONTEAGLE. Most likely – but in case it wasn't – isn't

CECIL. What do you think we should do about it?

MONTEAGLE. Me? Prorogue Parliament.

CECIL. Again?

MONTEAGLE. Well – that seems to be the focus of it – what I'm supposed to avoid.

CECIL. 'The terrible blow' – yes – Did the gunpowder get to Flanders?

MONTEAGLE. What gunpowder?

CECIL. The gunpowder you requisitioned from the royal arsenal under my seal

MONTEAGLE. As far as I know.

CECIL. As far as you know.

MONTEAGLE. It was due on a boat out of Gabriel's Wharf in March.

CECIL. How much was there?

MONTEAGLE. Three dozen barrels – something like that.

CECIL. And do you think that would be enough?

MONTEAGLE. To do what?

CECIL. William – who wrote this letter?

MONTEAGLE. I don't know.

CECIL. Who else has read it?

MONTEAGLE. Only my secretary – Thomas Winter.

Scene Two

PERCY, CATESBY, WINTER.

WINTER. He said it had been handed to him in the street – he said he'd lost his glasses and could I read it out to him.

PERCY. You should have let Fawkes stab Francis when you had the chance

CATESBY. Do you believe Monteagle?

WINTER. It wasn't Monty's hand – and it wasn't Francis'

PERCY. So he disguised it – what's it matter – we're fucked

CATESBY. There was no mention of powder?

WINTER. No – a blow they would not see

CATESBY. could mean anything

WINTER. and telling Monteagle to avoid Parliament

PERCY. Why in hell's name did you let him walk?

CATESBY. Because a man who will not keep his oath does not belong within our ranks.

FAWKES *arrives.*

Well?

FAWKES. The cellar's not been opened.

PERCY. How do you know?

FAWKES. I know. No footprints – nothing moved – the powder's dry.

PERCY. I'll go to Northumberland

CATESBY. No.

PERCY. the cellar's in my name

CATESBY. No.

PERCY. if there's anything amiss, they'll detain / me and

FAWKES. They'll strip the flesh from your bones until you give them names.

PERCY. I'd cut out my tongue first.

CATESBY. I'll do it for you. We talk to nobody until it is finished.

WINTER. We can't go on.

PERCY. Whatever – we have to silence Tresham

CATESBY. Perce, if Francis wanted to betray us, don't you think he'd have gone straight to Cecil himself? I don't believe Francis did this – the letter's vague – you said it yourself, Tom – whoever wrote it has only partial knowledge – and shows no desire that we should cease

WINTER. If Cecil's deciphered it – it's suicide

CATESBY. Martyrdom is the word, Tom – and perhaps that is the destiny God has granted us.

WINTER. We should vote.

CATESBY. What the hell do you think this is, Tom – a debating chamber?

WINTER. What about Jack, Kit, the others in the Midlands – don't they deserve to know?

CATESBY. They are armed and ready – God has chosen us – to live and ring in a new dawn of His glory or die and light a fire in men's minds that will burn for ever.

Scene Three

JAMES, ANE, CECIL, LENNOX, PRIVY COUNCIL.

JAMES. My armour – where the feck's my armour, Es.

LENNOX *goes to get armour.*

I should have stayed in Sherwood – I should have stayed in fecking Scotland. You've searched the Palace?

CECIL. No.

JAMES. Why not in hell's name?

CECIL. We should not be too hasty

JAMES. They're trying to annihilate me – me, ma Annie, ma family, ma government – hasty's too slow

CECIL. Supposing we search the Palace now – always assuming we have understood the letter correctly – what might we find – some gunpowder – and that is what we will have – no names – no heads – just gunpowder

TOPCLIFFE *enters.*

TOPCLIFFE. There's a room in Old Palace Yard let to Thomas Percy

JAMES. the Papist

CECIL. it would be best not to jump to conclusions

JAMES. I told you – all along I told you – Toleration –
Topcliffe, call the militia – I want every Papist within forty
miles in the Tower. Make that a hundred miles. Feck it,
every Papist in England.

CECIL. No.

JAMES. That's the royal command, Topcliffe.

CECIL. No.

JAMES. I am the King of England.

CECIL. Then act like one.

JAMES. Give me any reason why I don't string you up here
and now – On your watch a Papist assassin rents a room in
Parliament with the intention of blowing – oh aye and who
insisted I come back to London in the first place – what is
it, beagle? Being Secretary's not good enough – fancy a
shot at the top dog?

CECIL. If you want to reign over a blasted heath, howling at
the last few savages left to hear – then send out the militia.
You'll begin a war that will never end – and history will
write you down as the King who caused England to devour
herself.

JAMES. So what would you do, beagle?

CECIL. Wait – until London brims with every kind of
parliamentary creature – the taverns thick with dreams of
power and influence – when every lardy-arse lord and
Janus-faced gentleman has in his imagination set himself
down in that chamber – then we will tell the news – how the
King, by a divine inspiration, unlocked the riddle that had
mystified all others and led a search of Parliament himself.

We see FAWKES *laying the train of gunpowder underneath
Parliament.*

God's work – a sign that He intends you for His own – they
will be lighting bonfires in your memory for a thousand
years – Parliament will be at your feet – and every Catholic
in England will have melted into air.

LENNOX *arrives with the King's armour.*

JAMES. Where's Northumberland?

CECIL. I didn't call him.

Scene Four

PERCY *comes to* NORTHUMBERLAND, *who is limping. Elsewhere,* LENNOX *is still trying to buckle* JAMES *into his armour.*

N'LAND. You're up late.

PERCY. I suddenly remembered – I had some money you lent me.

N'LAND. It could have waited

PERCY. I thought you might need it – y'know – Parliament tomorrow – expensive business.

N'LAND. Thank you.

Beat.

PERCY. They say there'll be new legislation – that it will get worse.

N'LAND. They may try.

JAMES (*to* LENNOX). Get off me, you great nonce. Annie – you do it.

PERCY. Do you still have that letter? – the one I brought from Scotland – promising toleration.

N'LAND. Why, Thomas?

PERCY. Maybe it's time to remind the King of his promise.

N'LAND. Go home. You're right – there'll be a battle in this Parliament – and this time it will be a battle – because Englishmen will not stand by and see their countrymen persecuted for their faith – it's a battle we may yet win – this is not the moment to call the King a liar.

Beat.

PERCY. You'll sit tomorrow?

N'LAND. I'll be there – don't worry.

PERCY. But you're not well / – you should send a deputy

N'LAND. My mind is well enough – and I would trust no
deputy with this cause.

PERCY. What is it?

N'LAND. You're sweating.

PERCY. It means nothing – it's just the way God made me.

He goes. ANE *is now strapping* JAMES *into his armour.*

WINTER *in his lodging.*

WINTER. I dreamt tonight that all our barrels stood in the
Palace, the Lords and Commons gathered round. We came
in – you made a speech, Cat – full of fire and fury – and lit
the train.

In the cellar, FAWKES *lights the train of powder.*

The flame ran – and then nothing. And we stood there – like
we were naked and England laughing at us.

CECIL *kicks out the train of powder.* FAWKES *fights, is
grabbed.*

JAMES. Let me look at him. Who are you?

FAWKES. John Johnson – I am Thomas Percy's servant. Who
are you?

JAMES. Get him out – the man's possessed – Get him out!

FAWKES *is taken away.* CECIL *presents a paper to*
JAMES.

You need my permission to torture him?

CECIL. Legally.

JAMES *signs.*

Take this to Topcliffe, Monteagle – it'll be an education for
you.

MONTEAGLE *goes.*

WINTER *comes to* CATESBY *and* PERCY.

WINTER. Fawkes is taken.

CATESBY. He won't talk.

PERCY. He's a hired hand.

CATESBY. He's a soldier of Christ.

WINTER. Talk or not – we are undone.

CATESBY. No – we must ride.

WINTER. Where?

PERCY. Into the mouth of hell.

CATESBY. An army waits for us in the Midlands

WINTER. They'll be gone – the moment they know Westminster has failed, they'll run into the hills.

CATESBY. Why should they know we've failed – and while all eyes are on London we can still strike.

Scene Five

Thunder and lightning. FAWKES *appears suspended high over the stage, spread on a rack. Elsewhere,* GARNET *appears, kneels down and removes his shirt – he prays confusedly.*

FAWKES. 'You shall stand before kings and magistrates, and a brother shall betray his brother to death, and the father the son. And whoever persevers to the end shall be saved. And he that overcomes shall sit upon my throne, even as I have overcome and sit upon the throne of my father.'

Lightning. GARNET *flails himself* – FAWKES *screams.*

TOPCLIFFE *reports to* CECIL.

TOPCLIFFE. John Johnson, servant to Thomas Percy.

CECIL. Come on, Dicky – we need names

TOPCLIFFE. We're trying to find where the powder came from.

CECIL. Why – in the name of Beelzebub?

TOPCLIFFE. Because if it came from abroad – let's say Flanders – it'd be a breach of the Treaty

CECIL. And then what? We go back to war with Spain? No –
leave the powder to me – just get me some names – English
names. Have you got Percy yet?

TOPCLIFFE. No – but we know he was at Harry's yesterday.

Lightning. GARNET *flails himself* – FAWKES *screams.*

CECIL *meets* NORTHUMBERLAND.

CECIL. It's suspicious to say the least. A member of a Papist
plot comes to you, his relative, the night before and doesn't
mention it. We know they were warning their friends.

N'LAND. I am not a traitor – And you have no evidence this
was a Catholic plot.

CECIL. Actually it's the only thing Mr Johnny Johnson has
given us so far. And what I'm asking is – once they'd
blasted England back into the Middle Ages, whom were
they going to make King?

N'LAND. Percy asked me for the letter in which James
promised toleration.

CECIL. Is there such a letter?

N'LAND. I gave it to you.

CECIL. I've no memory of it – or circumstances in which His
Majesty would have offered toleration to enemies of the
state. I can check the files – things do go astray – for
example, no one can find any record of Thomas Percy ever
swearing allegiance. I'm sorry, Harry.

Lightning. GARNET *flails himself* – FAWKES *screams.*

CATESBY, WINTER *and* PERCY *come to* JACK *and* KIT
waiting at Holbeach House.

CATESBY. Liberty! Freedom! Tyranny is dead! Where the
fuck is everybody?

JACK. Lighting bonfires for the King's deliverance.

KIT. A posthorse from London rode through an hour since.

JACK. Where's Tresham?

PERCY. Gone to hell.

WINTER. He didn't show in London.

CATESBY. Come on – we need to get this powder inside – or it'll be no use

PERCY. Use for what, Cat – it's over.

CATESBY. No – it's never over – not even after death – that is what the resurrection means.

Lightning. GARNET *flails himself* – FAWKES *screams.*

TOPCLIFFE *reports to* CECIL.

TOPCLIFFE. It's Fawkes.

CECIL. Guido?

TOPCLIFFE. So there's our Spanish connection

CECIL. He's as English as you, Dicky. Sapper Fawkes. So they moled their way in

TOPCLIFFE. No sign of any tunnelling.

CECIL. Come on, work with me on this, Toppers – A known radical rents a room in Westminster and fills it with gunpowder? – I don't think. They dug a mine under the Palace – by night – dumped the slurry in the Thames

TOPCLIFFE. the walls are nine foot thick

CECIL. so it was the devil's own work to get through – they undermined Parliament – Can he write?

TOPCLIFFE. He could sign his name.

CECIL. Then write it up for him.

A rumble of thunder. FAWKES *is slowly lowered.*
GARNET*'s hands are shaking so much he cannot continue.*

TOPCLIFFE. There are reports from the Midlands – five men holed up on the Staffordshire border – descriptions fit the names Fawkes has given us – Catesby, Winter, Percy, the Wrights – oh, Tresham turned up in a whorehouse on Cheapside.

CECIL. Francis Tresham?

TOPCLIFFE. He was on Fawkes' list. And there's a Jesuit – Fawkes knew him as Farmer.

CECIL. Bingo.

Scene Six

Thunder, faint. Rain.

ANNE VAUX *comforts* GARNET.

CATESBY, WINTER, PERCY, JACK, KIT *holed at up at Holbeach.*

MARTHA *and* EDWARD *at home.*

SINGER. *Agnus Dei, qui tolis peccata mundi.*

PERCY. There is no finer sight than England at dusk – look at her – her soft hillsides stroked by mist

JACK. If I were Martha, I'd be jealous.

PERCY. I told her once – 'Martha, I love England more than I love you – more than Edward'

EDWARD. Is my father a traitor, Mother?

MARTHA. Yes

PERCY. God walked in those hills – rested at our hearth

EDWARD. A traitor is one that swears and then lies – and he must be hanged.

MARTHA. Yes, Edward

EDWARD. Who must hang them?

MARTHA. The honest men.

PERCY. and what England shall our children inherit – where a conscience is valued like wheat

EDWARD. Then the liars and swearers are fools, for there are liars and swearers enough to beat the honest men and hang up them.

PERCY. He shook this hand – he shook this bloody hand

SINGER. *miserere nobis.*

LIZZIE *stands before* CECIL.

CECIL. Does your husband know you are here, Lady Monteagle?

LIZZIE. No.

CECIL. What is it then? – this news you think is worth your traitorous brother's head.

LIZZIE. I can tell you where to find Father Garnet.

CECIL. And you consider that fair measure?

LIZZIE. Give me your word Francis will not be executed – lock him up for the rest of his life if you want – he did not begin it – this was not his doing

CECIL. Shh – you have my word, your brother will not die on the gallows.

LIZZIE. Garnet is at Anne Vaux's house – in the fireplace in her bedchamber – there's a wooden panel blackened to look like soot on stone.

She goes.

SINGER. *Agnus dei*

CATESBY. Do you think it's possible, Tom, to taste the Kingdom of Heaven on earth?

CECIL. Monty – are you there?

MONTEAGLE *emerges to* CECIL.

Take this (*A phial.*) – put it in a bottle of wine and go down to Francis' cell – he'll be ever so pleased to see you. When you've done that, we'll be about ready to declare you the man of the moment.

SINGER. *qui tolis peccata mundi*

CATESBY. There are moments, aren't there – in life – when time stops – which feel for a moment like eternity.

WINTER. But they're not eternal – not in this life.

CATESBY. And in heaven they will be? Is that what heaven will be?

WINTER. In Revelation the Angel swears that time will be no more.

CATESBY. But only after the apocalypse – the hail of blood, the burning mountains cast into the sea, plagues and darkness

SINGER. *miserere nobis.*

In the Palace, JAMES, *wrapped in the Union flag.* ANE.
The Dodo. JAMES *carries a gun.*

JAMES. Do you love me, Annie?

ANE. You are my husband.

JAMES. Aye but do you love me?

ANE. You are my king.

JAMES. It's all right – if you want to sleep with other men, I
mean – I do – we have an heir now – and one to spare.

SINGER. *Agnus Dei*

JAMES. Do you?

ANE. What, Your Majesty?

JAMES. Do you sleep with other men? No – don't answer that.
Do you love God?

ANE. Of course.

SINGER. *qui tolis peccata mundi*

PERCY. They're here.

KIT *begins to pray the Salve Regina.*

JAMES. We all love God – don't we, Annie. Everybody loves
God and nobody loves the King. My father tried to stab me
in the womb. They killed him with powder – blew him
ballack-naked from his bed. My first lover wanted to kill me
too – locked me in a tower – forced me to unspeakable
barbarity.

CATESBY. All that we have done has been in honour of the
Cross and of the True Faith

JAMES. The Catholics invented it – gunpowder – though the
Protestants are no better – Buchanan thrashed me – an
anointed king bent over the schoolbench like some pauper

CATESBY. Since it is God's will we should not succeed, let us
not be afraid to die

JAMES. all I wanted was an end to the violence – Rex
pacificus – d'you ken?

CATESBY. stand by me, Tom – and we will dine together in
paradise.

JAMES. a little peace to call ma ain.

SINGER. *dona nobis pacem.*

> *The Dodo calls 'Pax'.* JAMES *aims at it. Fires. Shots ring out all round.* CATESBY, PERCY, WINTER, JACK *and* KIT *die.*

Scene Seven

And there is only CECIL *and* GARNET – *his hands bloody and battered. Very bright light.*

CECIL. Can I get you anything – a drink – food – a chair?

GARNET. I wish to speak to the King – I am his loyal subject and had no part in this conspiracy.

CECIL. You didn't authorise it?

GARNET. I gave them no authority. The King will understand this – because we are under the same accusation as his mother – persecuted for our faith under a false charge of treason

CECIL. And the King will listen to you, will he?

GARNET. The King is a man of conscience. I will tell him what I have long said – give us the liberty you have promised and I will order every Jesuit out of England tomorrow.

CECIL. But would they go? Does anybody listen to you? Catesby, didn't. If you have any authority you're guilty at least by negligence – if you don't, your assurance is worthless. Oh – and about the King and his sainted mother. He killed her. He didn't wield the axe or sign the warrant – but do you honestly think we would have done it without his consent? He winked at it – in return for an English crown. So let's leave faith and conscience out of this – the charge is treason

GARNET. the way of every tyrant since Pilate

CECIL. in England we do not kill people for their conscience

GARNET. and in Scythia they do not rip the bodies of innocent men while they breathe and toss their entrails on the fire

CECIL. don't talk to me about cruelty. I have an orrery – in the great hall at Hatfield – the heavens arrayed in matchless splendour – by day the planets dance within their spheres, by night the ceiling luminous with stars. The mind behind this clockwork miracle is a Spanish Jew – the only one of his kin to escape the Inquisition.

GARNET. You have no evidence to try me for treason.

CECIL. We have a signed confession that says otherwise.

GARNET. Then it was obtained under torture, not under oath.

CECIL. 'At Christmas we met at Robert Catesby's lodging in Lambeth, where Father Farmer (aka Garnet aka Perkins aka Waley etc) confirmed that it was lawful to kill innocents in a just cause. He then gave us Communion. Lady Vaux was present throughout.' We have Lady Vaux in custody – will she deny this?

GARNET. I was not talking of the plot – I had no knowledge of it then.

CECIL. When did you?

GARNET. I may not say.

CECIL. We can torture you again if it'd help – if it would bring you closer to your Saviour.

GARNET. I may not say.

CECIL. Spin me an equivocation then – tell me you knew nothing until the bonfires began to celebrate the King's deliverance?

GARNET. That would be a lie, not an equivocation.

CECIL. The difference being?

GARNET. Its chief purpose would be to save my own skin.

CECIL. So you did know about this plot before?

GARNET. I may not say.

CECIL. Do you know what day it is?

GARNET. St Sebastian's – or near it.

CECIL. A martyr for every day in the calendar.

GARNET. Not every day, no.

CECIL. Still space for you then.

GARNET. I hope only for a place in heaven.

CECIL. And where would you have me go?

GARNET. I would have all souls turn to God and find their true home.

CECIL. And yet you would have blown me into dust with all my sins upon me.

GARNET. I did not authorise this deed.

CECIL. Will Anne Vaux be in heaven with you – sitting at your feet? Or on your knee?

GARNET. My relationship with Lady Vaux is without shame.

CECIL. her white hand under your vestments

GARNET. you are vile

CECIL. Nothing arouses England like lechery coupled with religion – the sanctified arse bumping between the virgin thighs – the ecstatic crucifixion of the beast – I don't believe these things, of course / – But it is what people say

GARNET. I doubt you believe in anything.

CECIL. Did you sodomise her? All the rage in the seminaries – 'Taking it like a Jesuit' – on your knees with the devil behind you

GARNET. Why do you think England has the same rancid imagination as you?

CECIL. Because you were found in her bedroom, you foolish old goat.

Beat.

GARNET. Yes – I knew about the plot. I had no part in its invention or execution – but I knew about it.

CECIL. What did you know?

GARNET. I knew there was gunpowder underneath the Palace – I knew they intended to blow up the King and the government.

CECIL. And you approved.

GARNET. No.

CECIL. You told no one – you warned no one

GARNET. I could not – I was bound by the seal of confession

CECIL. which should tie your tongue for all time

GARNET. yes

CECIL. but now you've told me. So to protect some woman's reputation you'd break a bond you held more sacred than your loyalty to your King.

GARNET. The penitent permitted me to break the seal if I was tortured – which you have done.

CECIL. I do believe in something by the way. My garden. I have faith the seed I scatter – will grow. I tend it, I water it – and when I die I shall feed it with my flesh. Not a bad religion – gives me a sense of place in the cosmos – preferable to all those supernatural battles with mankind as cannon fodder – or like spectators at a play. From dust we are made and to dust we shall return – and behind us we shall leave orreries and gardens and the memories of gardens, and the memory of terror. We shall have to hang you now.

GARNET. You would have done so anyway – my free admission can only improve my credit and I hope thereby that of my Church.

CECIL. It is expedient that one should die to save the people.

GARNET. Your words.

CECIL. And when England learns that it was through confession – men dabbling in divine absolution – that we came within a heartbeat of anarchy – do you think we shall need to suppress Rome any longer in this land? She must have been one godalmighty fuck.

GARNET. Humility, honour, obedience – every virtue needful to good government is enshrined in the Holy Mother Church. Take away this authority – how will you govern?

CECIL. The way the Church has since Moses – by the Law

GARNET. and what authority has the Law without God?

CECIL. The authority of the King / – and then men's duty and conscience

GARNET. And what authority has the King without God? And what is man's conscience and duty without God? Unless we suffer for our misdeeds – unless we are rewarded – unless there is terror and there is beauty not only for a time – but for all time? You believe in your garden – another in his wealth and another in the power of his sword – who's right? When men believe anything, they'll soon believe nothing – and your garden will be left a wilderness of tigers.

CECIL. Christ died – and if I were Pilate I would have killed him – and slept easy – perhaps not so publicly – a knife in an alley – a brawl over a bill – but you never can predict how these things will play. It's only the symbols that matter. We'll hang you between heaven and earth, as unworthy of both, cut off your genitals because you are unfit to leave any generation behind you, the bowels that conceived your treachery will be thrown on the fire, the head which imagined it, cut off. / And then your dismembered quarters will be exposed to the fowls of the air

Swelling music drowns out CECIL.

JAMES *appears – addressing the nation before a large Union flag.*

JAMES. . . . I should be very sorry if any innocent should receive blame or harm for this attempt. For although it cannot be denied that it was the blind superstition of their religion that drove them on – it does not follow that all professing their religion are guilty. Although no other sect of heretics – no, not Turk, Jew, Pagan, even those who worship the divil – did ever maintain by the grounds of their religion that it was lawful – even meritorious (as Roman Catholics call it) to murther princes. Yet let us not act rashly, for Catholics too may be honourable men . . .

GARNET *is hung, drawn and quartered.*

ELLESMERE *reports to* CECIL.

ELLESMERE. Parliament has voted him three subsidies and six fifteenths and tenths.

CECIL. What's that in new money?

ELLESMERE. about 450 grand a year

CECIL. What they gave Bess to fight a war with Spain. Teddy, I think we can call that a job well done.

ELLESMERE. Just as well – because there's not a recusant to be found

A cheer like a great wave.

ANNE VAUX *carries a handkerchief bundled up in her fist.*

ANNE VAUX. When they cut up his body – a young man – eager to obtain a drop of his holy blood – ran forward to the block. And as the head was cast into the basket a husk of corn flew up into the young man's hand – and seeing there was blood on it – he rejoiced. (*Unwrapping the handkerchief.*) Some days later, perusing it more closely he perceived a face, perfect as if it had been painted. (*She holds up the tiniest husk.*) Henry.

CECIL. What's this?

ELLESMERE. It's a bill – for the ironwork to fix Catesby and Percy's heads to London Bridge, twenty-three shilling sixpence

ANNE VAUX. For so the Lord will use the meanest creatures to manifest His glory – and by stones and straw brings comfort to His servants.

CECIL. Pay him twenty.

End.